Epworth Commentaries

General Editor
Ivor H. Jones

The Epistle to the Galatians

Epworth Commentaries

The Epistle to the
GALATIANS

JOHN ZIESLER

EPWORTH PRESS

ISBN 0 7162 0486 X

First Published 1992
by Epworth Press
1 Central Buildings Westminster
London SW1H 9NR

Typeset by Regent Typesetting, London
and printed in Finland by
Werner Söderström Oy

CONTENTS

GENERAL INTRODUCTION

The *Epworth Preacher's Commentaries* that Greville P. Lewis edited so successfully in the 1950s and 1960s having now served their turn, the Epworth Press has commissioned a team of distinguished academics who are also preachers and teachers to create a new series of commentaries that will serve the 1990s and beyond. We have seized the opportunity offered by the publication in 1989 of the Revised English Bible to use this very readable and scholarly version as the basis of our commentaries, and we are grateful to the Oxford and Cambridge University Presses for the requisite licence and for granting our authors pre-publication access. They will nevertheless be free to cite and discuss other translations wherever they think that these will illuminate the original text.

Just as the books that make up the Bible differ in their provenance and purpose, so our authors will necessarily differ in the structure and bearing of their commentaries. But they will all strive to get as close as possible to the intention of the original writers, expounding their texts in the light of the place, time, circumstances, and culture that gave them birth, and showing why each work was received by Jews and Christians into their respective Canons of Holy Scripture. They will seek to make full use of the dramatic advance in biblical scholarship world-wide but at the same time to explain technical terms in the language of the common reader, and to suggest ways in which Scripture can help towards the living of a Christian life today. They will endeavour to produce commentaries that can be used with confidence in ecumenical, multiracial, and multifaith situations, and not by scholars only but by preachers, teachers, students, church members, and anyone who wants to improve his or her understanding of the Bible.

Ivor H. Jones

PREFACE

The text followed in this commentary is that of the Revised English Bible (REB) which is not printed in full, but the italic type indicates where quotations from it are being made. The comment is taken section by section, aiming to make sense of the passages as wholes. Inevitably there are matters of dispute and some relatively technical questions, but as far as possible these have not been allowed to interrupt the general comment. Instead, they are grouped after each general comment, verse by verse. Scholars are hopelessly addicted to footnotes, but there has been an honest attempt to use them only to inform the reader where further discussion or other useful material may be found.

Inevitably, there are critical issues in the study of Galatians. It is not normally doubted that Paul wrote it, but there is dispute about who and more precisely where the Galatians were, about whether it is a very early Pauline letter indeed or to be dated near the time of the writing of Romans, and about the relationship between Acts 15 and the so-called Council of Jerusalem, and the meeting Paul describes in Gal. 2. These matters are not discussed in the Introduction, which is aimed instead at what might be called reader-orientation. The critical questions are given a brief treatment in Essay II at the end of the commentary. Where they impinge on the understanding of the letter they will be mentioned at the appropriate points, but often a decision on these issues is not essential to the non-specialist reader (or any other). By relegating them to the end, the author hopes that the reader can get as quickly as possible to the text of the letter, but with enough orientation to assist understanding.

At this point I must express my indebtedness to all those scholars – by no means all named in the book – who have helped me to study this letter, but also to those students at the University of Bristol with whom I worked through Galatians. Who was teaching whom is a nice question.

ABBREVIATIONS

This list does not include abbreviations for books of the Bible or of the Apocrypha.

II *Apoc. Bar.*	the Syriac Apocalypse of Baruch
I Clem.	the letter of St. Clement of Rome
Josephus, *Ant.*	the Antiquities of Josephus
JSNT	Journal for the Study of the New Testament
Jub.	the Book of Jubilees
LXX	the Septuagint (the Greek translation of the Old Testament and Apocrypha)
MS(S)	Manuscript(s)
NT	New Testament
NT	*Novum Testamentum* (a journal published in the Netherlands)
NTS	*New Testament Studies*
OT	Old Testament
PssSol.	the Psalms of Solomon
1QS	the Rule of the Community from Qumran
1QM	the War Scroll from Qumran
1QH	the Thanksgiving Hymns from Qumran
1QpHab	the Commentary on Habakkuk from Qumran
REB	the Revised English Bible
TDNT	the One-Volume *Theological Dictionary of the New Testament*, ed. G. Kittel and G. Friedrich, translated and abridged by G. W. Bromiley, Eerdmans/Paternoster 1985.

A NOTE ON BOOKS

Although many books, including commentaries on Galatians and on other New Testament writings, have influenced this commentary either directly or indirectly, they are much too numerous to list. However, six works which are often cited deserve special mention:

J. M. G. Barclay, *Obeying the Truth*, T. & T. Clark 1988, cited as Barclay, *Truth*;
H. D. Betz, *Galatians* (Hermeneia Series), Fortress 1979;
P. Bonnard, *L'Épître de Saint Paul aux Galates*, Delachaux et Niestlé ² 1972;
F. F. Bruce, *The Epistle to the Galatians*, Paternoster 1982;
C. B. Cousar, *Galatians* (Interpretation Commentaries), John Knox Press 1982;
B. M. Metzger, *A Textual Commentary on the Greek New Testament*, United Bible Societies 1971.

ALL COMMENTARIES ARE REFERRED TO BY THE AUTHOR'S NAME ALONE.

Anyone wishing to pursue the study of Galatians further could start with one of the above (though Metzger is for advanced students only). However, the author's strong recommendation is to read Barclay, *Truth*, and the forthcoming *Galatians* by J. D. G. Dunn, A. & C. Black.

Other commentaries of historical importance, or occasionally referred to, include:

J. Bligh, *Galatians*, St Paul Publications 1969;
R. Bring, *Commentary on Galatians*, Muhlenberg 1961;
E. D. Burton, *The Epistle to the Galatians*, (ICC), T. & T. Clark 1921;
R. Y. K. Fung, *The Epistle to the Galatians*, Eerdmans 1988;
K. Grayston, *Galatians and Philippians*, Epworth 1957;
M. J. Lagrange, *Saint Paul, Épître aux Galates*, J. Gabalda ²1925;
J. B. Lightfoot, *Saint Paul's Epistle to the Galatians*, Macmillan ¹⁰1890;

H. Schlier, *Der Brief an die Galater*, Vandenhoeck & Ruprecht 1949.

Perspectives on Paul have changed considerably in the last fifteen years (see the Introduction), and older works will obviously not reflect this change.

INTRODUCTION

There is nothing bogus about Paul's letter to the Galatians: it really is a letter and not a theological treatise dressed up in the form of a letter. At least in the first instance therefore, the reader is not sitting down to study an ancient piece of theology, but is listening in to one end of a conversation and a very heated conversation at that. It is true that not many modern readers of Galatians have a burning interest in rediscovering past controversies; more probably they are reading to discover what the letter has to say to them now. Nevertheless this commentary is written out of the conviction that the best way to let the letter speak to people today is to help them to put themselves first in the position of the original readers – or hearers – and as far as possible hear what they heard all those centuries ago. The application of the letter's message to ourselves and our church and our society must come, but is better achieved by working through its original impact than by ignoring it. Moreover, any modern impact may well be left to the reader to experience and not be dictated by a commentator. Nevertheless the commentator too is a modern reader, and from time to time, but especially in Essay I at the end of the commentary proper, more than half an eye is directed at what the letter may mean for us today. Yet it remains the case that the primary aim of this commentary is to bring an ancient controversy alive, and with it Paul's message to the Galatians.

Perhaps ideally a commentary would simply work through the letter, letting its purport emerge as we go along. In practice, however, in most cases (and certainly in the case of Galatians) it helps a good deal to have before we start some notion of what it is all about and also some idea of what sort of writing (what *genre*) we are reading. The danger then is that we draw our conclusions in advance of looking at the evidence, but the advantage is that we avoid too much initial mystification.

What Galatians is about

One of the oddities of this letter is that we are not told in so many words what the issue is until 5.2, namely that the Gentile Galatian Christians are being urged to submit to circumcision, though from 2.3 onwards it becomes increasingly clear that this must be the issue. There have been many theories as to who was pressing circumcision on them and why, and there has been some disagreement as to whether just circumcision, together with Sabbath observance and the keeping of Jewish food laws, was being urged upon them, or whether it was understood on both sides that circumcision must lead to the observance of the whole of the Torah (the law of Moses). We shall be considering such matters as we go through the letter. Yet what has given rise to the problem is clear enough: it is whether when Gentiles become Christians they have to accept circumcision and what it entails in order to be full members of the people of God. Paul's argument is that to be acceptable to God (to put it in individualist terms) and to be within the one people of God (to put it in community terms) one thing and one thing alone is both necessary and sufficient: faith in Jesus Christ. To put the same matter in another way, one does not need to become a Jew in order to become a Christian. If the church were to require circumcision and with that the keeping of the Torah, that would be tantamount to saying on the one hand that Christ and faith in him are not sufficient, and to saying on the other hand that the gospel is not really for all people without qualification, but only for those who are or are prepared to become Jews. In Paul's view, it seems, this would make Christ less than central and the gospel less than universal.

If we accept that it is not important that all Christians should observe the Torah (and we must note that Paul never says that Jewish Christians ought to cease observing it), does this leave a predominantly Gentile Christian community without moral guidance? Whether or not his opponents raised this question, Paul sees it as an issue to be faced, and he faces it in chapter 5. There he maintains that the gift of the Spirit leads the community into a way of life that is good, and not just moral, for some of the aspects of the good and virtuous life that are set out as fruits of the Spirit are things to which the law cannot apply: it is hard, for example, to see how there could ever be a law about joy. At all events, those Christians who are not committed to Torah-keeping are not therefore left without guidance or standards, far from it.

Such an outline of the issue in Galatians would be regarded by many modern Pauline scholars as pretty run of the mill. Yet until the work of K. Stendahl[1] and E. P. Sanders[2], followed since by many others, a quite different account would probably have been given. This quite different account would have had Paul opposing Jewish 'legalism', by which was meant the idea that by keeping Torah or simply by doing good deeds, one could earn acceptance with God. Stendahl showed that in Galatians Paul was more concerned with the community question (do I have to become a Jew in order to be a Christian?) than with individual acceptance with God (how can I find a gracious God?). Sanders showed that in Jewish texts early enough to be relevant, no authority taught that God's approval was to be earned, nor that salvation was by human merit. On the contrary, in Judaism up to Paul's time salvation was always by God's grace, and the law was the divine guidance for those who had already been accepted as his people. Moreover, argued Sanders, Paul's letters show no evidence that he was opposing such a merit-centred view of salvation; his resistance to the imposition of the Torah on Gentile Christians was for the two reasons already noted, namely that faith in Christ is by itself sufficient, and that the gospel is for Jews and Gentiles equally and universally. If the views of Stendahl and Sanders are accepted, then it is no longer possible to read Galatians as an attack on self-righteousness or the attempt to accumulate merit before God. The questions this shift of understanding raise for the church's use of Galatians are discussed in Essay I.

The form of Galatians

We have already said that Galatians is a real letter, but what sort of a letter it is is a matter for dispute. The important commentary by H. D. Betz (1979) proposes that its *genre* is that of the 'apologetic letter' and that its basic structure is as follows (Betz uses Latin terms, but rough English equivalents are here substituted):

1.1–5	Letter Prescript
1.6–11	Introduction
1.12–2.14	Narration of the facts at issue
2.15–21	Proposition (matters of agreement and disagreement, and basic theses)
3.1–4.31	Confirmation (development of the basic theses)
5.1–6.10	Exhortation
6.11–18	Letter Postscript

COMMENTARY

Prescript (or salutation)
1–5

The ancient letter-writing etiquette was different from ours. The usual way of beginning was with the name of the writer or sender, then the name of the recipient, followed by a word of greeting. So here, except that characteristically Paul fills out the address with theological matter. After his name, he gives his self-description as *an apostle*, one especially *commissioned by God*, and no merely human or merely ecclesiastical emissary. To judge from what follows in chapter 1, this was something on which he wished (needed?) to insist: his authorization did not come from the Jerusalem apostles or from the Twelve, but directly from God himself and from *Jesus Christ*. One way of attacking Paul's version of Christianity would be to question his credentials, and before he launches into the controversy Paul here gives notice that his credentials cannot be doubted. He is no second-hand apostle.

In all his letter-openings Paul makes reference to *God* as *Father* and here the reference is accompanied by him *who raised him* (Jesus) *from the dead*. The God whom Paul worships is thus defined both as Father and as life-giver. The recipients are *the churches of Galatia*. It is not certain whether these Galatian Christians inhabit the old kingdom of Galatia, roughly speaking a large area of central Asia Minor centred on what is now Ankara, or whether they inhabit the Roman province of the same name which covered a much wider area, including the southern areas of Pisidia and Lycaonia (of which Derbe and Lystra were cities). If they lived in the old kingdom, then it is quite likely that they were Celts ('Gaul', 'Gaelic' and 'Galatia' are all from the same root) though doubtless the population was quite mixed. Although a decision on this matter is important for the reconstruction of the history of Paul and his mission, it has to remain tangential to the understanding of the letter. See Essay II.

The greeting *Grace to you and peace* may well amount to turning a formal salutation into a blessing. Paul uses not *chairete* or *chairein*,

1

common words of greeting, but *charis* ('grace'), a word with somewhat flexible use but which in Paul's letters generally and presumably here in particular means God's undeserved favour, to be seen especially in Jesus Christ (e.g. 1.6, 15; 5.4; 6.18). *Peace* in the Bible commonly denotes not just the absence of conflict nor is it just an assurance that one does not have a dagger in one's hand. More positively it stands for total well being with and under God, cf. 5.22; 6.16. It is an objective state and not merely a subjective feeling of being at peace with God. Together, the two words of greeting express a good deal of what the gospel is: the reception of God's favour and life within his bounty. Once again we note that *God* is *Father*, but we also learn that *Jesus Christ* is *Lord* which means that the Christian community has its existence within his power and authority.

This Lord *gave himself for our sins* (v. 4). This sounds rather like a formula that Paul is quoting, cf. 2.20; I Cor. 15.3; Mark 10.45. Unfortunately he does not explain what the formula means and how Christ's death affects our sins. It is not biblical to suppose that until Christ came sins could not be forgiven: one need think only of the ritual of the Day of Atonement in Lev. 16 and of psalms like Ps. 32. Is it that the death of Christ moves people to repentance, or is it that in some way that death provides a vehicle for forgiveness? Indeed is forgiveness the point at issue? The next part of v. 4 shows that the function of the sacrifice of Christ is not just forgiveness but *rescue*. People are under the power *of the present wicked age* and need to be liberated (saved) from it. Bringing to an end the power of evil forces over men and women is what Christ achieves. From this it is clear at the outset that though on the surface there is not much in Galatians of what we call eschatology, it is very much there in the background. In other words there is the well-known division of human and world history into two epochs: the old wicked age which is the world as hitherto known and experienced, and the new age of the reign cf God which has been inaugurated though not yet consummated in the death and resurrection of Christ. It is important to notice that here Paul does not say that the old wicked age/world has disappeared, rather that those who belong to Christ as Lord have been liberated from it. The old malign forces go on: we today may think of such things as greed, nationalism, fashion and materialism, rather than necessarily of superhuman agencies. Such things still exist and still dominate people's lives but it is no longer inevitable that they should, for a new way of life and freedom is now possible.

2

Finally we have an ascription of praise to God. Usually at this point in a letter Paul gives praise to God for the people to whom he is writing. Here he simply makes a general ascription.

* * * *

1.1 *apostle*: though this is a word for anyone who is 'sent', in the NT it can have a range of meanings.

(i)   In a mundane sense it can denote any emissary or messenger, as in Phil. 2.25.

(ii)   It can be used for the Twelve, as in Matt. 10.2; Mark 6.3.

(iii)   It can also be used for a wider group so as to include Paul and Barnabas (Acts 14.4, 14) and also James the brother of Jesus (Gal. 1.19; I Cor. 15.7) and many others unnamed (I Cor. 15:7 again).

It is widely supposed that the sense of the Greek *apostolos* is influenced by the use of its Hebrew equivalent to convey something like the idea of a plenipotentiary: the one sent is equivalent to the one who sent him (John 3.16, and in the Mishnah, *Berakoth* 5.5). It is evident from the present context that Paul is not claiming membership of a wider group (iii) on a par with Barnabas, but membership of a specially commissioned group on a par with Peter and others who were witnesses of the resurrection of Jesus, cf. 1.1, 18–19 and I Cor. 9.1; 15.8. He is not claiming membership of the Twelve, but he does seem to want to be in much the same category (ii). At all events he believes that his message is endorsed by God in that God directly commissioned him to preach to the Gentiles. If there is in this chapter more than a hint of defensiveness in his protestation of his genuinely apostolic credentials, it is because Paul is arguing that his authority and his message may indeed have received the endorsement of the Jerusalem church, but did not need that endorsement. His claim to direct divine commissioning is in line with that of the prophets, see Amos 7.14f.; Isa. 6.8ff.; Jer. 1.1–9.

1.2 *the churches of Galatia*: notice the plural. This is a circular letter, yet there was presumably only one copy which had to be taken around, not a large number of copies to be distributed. This is shown by the fact that the postscript (6.11–18) is in Paul's own large hand, something that would not show up in copies. We can hardly suppose that Paul laboriously added the postscript several times to different copies.

1.3 *God the Father and our Lord Jesus Christ*: there is a certain amount of confusion in the manuscripts (MSS) of Galatians at this point. There are two main options, either the text represented by REB or that indicated as a footnote, 'God our Father and the Lord Jesus Christ'. The latter is a more usual formula in Paul (Rom. 1.7; I Cor. 1.3; II Cor. 1.2; Phil. 1.2; Philemon 3). Did Paul write something a little different for once, but then copyists wrote what they expected to find, or did Paul use his normal expression and then copyists altered it to match the common expression 'our Lord Jesus Christ'? Readers may think it hardly matters, but editors of Greek texts and modern translations have to decide these things.

1.4 *gave himself for our sins*: this may reflect Jewish martyr theology, according to which the deaths of the righteous martyrs have a cleansing effect on the people. See for example II Macc. 7.32, 37f.[4] It is more likely that as elsewhere in Galatians (2.19f.; 6.14; see also 3.23–26; 4.1–9; 5.1) the death of Christ represents and indeed brings about the end of the old age, the old order, at least for those who belong to him and have faith in him. See also Rom. 6.5–11; 7.1–6; Col. 2.20; 3.3.

1.5 *glory*: the Greek word *doxa* can mean 'reputation', but in the Septuagint[5] it frequently translates a Hebrew word which can convey God's revealing and concealing himself at the same time. That is, as in the cloud over the Tabernacle (Ex. 40.34ff.) God's presence and power are indicated but veiled. In the NT Jesus Christ is the glory/ *doxa* of God, e.g. I Cor. 2.8; II Cor. 3.18; 4.4, 6; 8.23. Yet very often there seems to be a more vague reference to the divine splendour, or indeed to the ascription of praise to God as the recognition of that splendour. So here, *glory* is perhaps the recognition of the sheer Godness of God.

Introduction to the theme of the letter
1.6–10

In the absence of any expression of thanksgiving for the Galatians, Paul goes straight into a pained remonstrance with them for having succumbed to the blandishments of some unspecified people who have been trying to persuade them that the gospel as they have received it from Paul is not the full gospel. At this point he does not say what these people are proposing, but as the letter unfolds it becomes clear that they are arguing that to be truly the people of God, the Galatians need not only faith in Jesus Christ, but also circumcision, the time-honoured and hitherto virtually invariable means of entry to God's people. Circumcision is the rite of entry, but it represents acceptance of the obligations of Torah, the law of Moses, cf. 5.3 and Gen. 17.9–14.

However, the idea that anything other than faith in Christ is needed for belonging to the people of God is regarded by Paul as *a different gospel* which in reality is not *another gospel* but no gospel at all. To make any such further requirement is to *distort the gospel of Christ*. Paul does not here say what the gospel is, but is simply concentrating on his argument that to add anything to it is to pervert or destroy it. All who do attempt to pervert it in this way are to be placed under a ban or even a curse (note that here at the beginning of the letter we have ban or curse, literally *anathema*, while at the end, 6.16, blessing is invoked). For Paul the gospel spells blessing, while anything else spells curse. If we accept the meaning *banned*, then presumably Paul is saying that the troublemakers must be banned from the meetings of the churches.

It looks as if Paul has been accused of making things too easy for Gentile converts, for in v. 10 he defends himself against the charge of *asking for human approval*. Such a charge is understandable: to require male Gentile converts to be circumcised in adulthood would certainly be to ask them to suffer pain and – in the light of current surgical procedures – to run some risk. In Judaism itself, probably far more men became adherents of the synagogue than ever became full converts (proselytes), simply because for the latter circumcision was demanded.[6] Paul, however, denies that he is making things easy for people; if he had wanted to do that, he would not have been a Christian in the first place. All the same, we do not need much imagination to see that those who were themselves devoted followers of the Torah, and believed that the keeping of it was an essential mark of being God's covenant people, would regard as an easy option Paul's proposal that nothing should be demanded of Gentile Christians other than faith in Jesus Christ.

* * * *

1.6   *a different gospel*: it is not until 2.15–16 that we are told almost in so many words that the different gospel is one that demands observance of the law from Gentile converts, and not until 5.2f. that the insistence on circumcision is the trigger of the controversy. The REB footnote to this verse tells us that there is disagreement between MSS here. The basic issue is whether or not there is a specific reference to Christ in connection with grace. As such a reference is almost certainly implied anyway, the problem is hardly serious.

1.7   *some who unsettle your minds*: who were they? We have already noted that they were people who thought that faith in Christ, while necessary, was not sufficient for belonging to the people of God.

(i) They may have been Gentile Christians who had discovered by hearing the Old Testament or from their contacts with Jews (or Jewish Christians) that circumcision was the traditional rite of entry, perhaps without fully understanding the total obligation to the Torah that this entailed, 5.3; 6.13.[7]

(ii) Just possibly they may have been Gnostics who valued circumcision not for its connection with Torah but as a mystic rite for its own sake,[8] though it is hard to find evidence that Gnosticism was the problem in Galatia.

(iii) On the whole it is most likely that they were Jewish Christians, whether or not they taught with the authority of the Jerusalem church, who genuinely believed that Paul's gospel was incomplete. Later on in chapter 2 while Paul attacks Peter for his behaviour at Antioch, he is at pains to stress the approval he had received from the Jerusalem leaders, so on the whole it is unlikely that the troublemakers were official emissaries of that church.

1.8   *let him be banned* (also v. 9): the Greek is *anathema*. This is strong language indeed and conveys Paul's conviction that people with such views have no place in the churches. Violent language is a feature of this letter, see for example 3.1; 5.4, 12. Paul really believes that if these people have their way the gospel will not be the gospel.

Narration

1.11–2.14

There now follows a long section in which Paul states the facts which bear on the dispute. He includes his own endorsement by the Jerusalem leaders, an endorsement which on the one hand he wants to say he does not need, and which on the other hand supports his case. He then goes on to tell the story of what happened at Antioch, a story which bears so directly on the situation in Galatia that its narration has a double focus. The Antioch issue and the Galatian issue thus become almost inextricably intertwined.

How Paul became an apostle

1.11–24

We begin with autobiography, the purpose of which is to underline what was claimed in v. 1, namely that Paul's commissioning, and with that his presentation of the gospel, derives directly from Jesus Christ and from the God who raised him from the dead. Although elsewhere he is happy enough to be part of a chain of tradition (e.g. I Cor. 11.23ff.; 15.3ff.), here he is adamant that the gospel came to him unmediated by any human agency. It is possible though not certain that he refers to his experience on the road to Damascus when he says (v. 12) that his gospel was *received through a revelation of Jesus Christ*. He makes a considerable point of stressing that his zeal as a Jew, greater than that of most of his contemporaries (vv. 13–14), was what led him to persecute the infant Christian community. In that zeal he was affected by *the traditions of* his *ancestors*, which tells us that he was a Pharisee, devoted not just to the written Torah (in effect the Pentateuch) but also to its interpretation in oral tradition.

As already hinted in v. 1, he then places himself in the line of the

OT prophets in claiming that God had intended him for a particular mission, that of preaching among the *Gentiles* the good news of his *Son*, Jesus Christ (vv. 15–16). Both the revelation of that *Son* to Paul and his commission to *proclaim him among the Gentiles*, are here put at the same point.

Despite Acts 9 and the story of Ananias, Paul is emphatic that no one instructed him, that no one was his father or mother in the faith. For some unstated reason he *went off to Arabia* (v. 17) and at some unspecified time later *returned to Damascus*. He did *three years later* (v. 18) revisit *Jerusalem*, meet *Cephas* and *stay two weeks with him*. There is no account of what he was doing in Arabia or in the subsequent three years (assuming that they should not include the time in Arabia). There is equally no account of what he and Cephas (Peter) talked about during their fortnight together. They must surely have talked a good deal about the life and teachings of Jesus, yet there is astonishingly little explicit echo of such things in the letters. It is also astonishing that apart from Peter, Paul met only James the brother of Jesus: perhaps the former persecutor was still regarded with fear and suspicion, or perhaps the apostle to the Gentiles was already regarded as a dangerous radical (if he had begun his work at this time), or perhaps the other apostles were genuinely busy elsewhere. No one knows, but Paul heavily underlines that he met only Peter and James, *God knows I am not lying*, v. 20. The most obvious reason for his minimizing his contacts with the Jerusalem church is his wish to maintain his first-hand apostolate, and to rebut any idea that it is derived from or delegated by the 'real' apostles.

Thus, when he left Jerusalem *for the regions of Syria and Cilicia* (v. 21) *the Christian congregations in Judaea* had never met him (v. 22). They knew their *former persecutor* was now one of them (v. 23) and they praised God for it, and that was all.

* * * *

1.12 *I received it through a revelation of Jesus Christ*: but precisely what was revealed? We have noted that some things, like the semi-credal summary of the work of Jesus in I Cor. 15.3ff., clearly did come to him from tradition or were taught him, and common sense tells us that he must have known at least a modicum about the Christian movement in order to want to persecute it. Therefore it seems likely that what came as a revelation was his distinctive angle on the gospel, or at least the beginnings of it. In the light of v. 16 this distinctive angle must have centred on the mission to the Gentiles, and must surely also have included the denial of the need for male converts to be circumcised (though see below on 5.11). Whether it also included the fully developed theology of justification by faith apart from works of the law that we find in this letter is disputed. It is possible that the full development occurred only after the dispute at Antioch which we encounter in chapter 2, and was elaborated for the first time only in Galatians. It can also be held that at least in germ it was from the time of his call-conversion that Paul held the view of justification apart from the law that is set out here.[9]

1.13 *I persecuted the church of God*: for Paul as persecutor see also I Cor. 15.9; Phil. 3.6; I Tim. 1.13; Acts 8.1–3; 9.1–2, 4–5; 22.4–5, 7–8; 26.9–11, 14–15. It is a bit of a mystery where he operated as a persecutor. His Damascus persecution never happened as he met Christ on the way there, so presumably he operated in Judaea including Jerusalem. Yet according to v. 22 the Judaean Christians did not know him by sight. Perhaps he had been a shadowy figure who kept in the background, though that is hardly the picture given in Acts 8.1–3.

1.15 *who from my birth had set me apart*: for similar statements about the prophets see Jer. 1.5 and Isa. 49.1–6. It is literally 'from my mother's womb'.

who had called me through his grace: we noted in v. 3 that grace is for all Christians. That general grace must be included here, but there must also be something more: Paul's commission as apostle to the Gentiles (v. 16) is itself an act of divine generosity, just as God's accepting men and women into his people is an act of generosity. It can be argued that 'call' is a better word for what happened to Paul than 'conversion', for it is anachronistic to think that Paul was converted from one religion (Judaism) to another (Christianity). Indeed it can well be maintained that Paul saw the Christian gospel as the true and fulfilled form of Judaism, and not an alternative to it. Yet in the basic sense of a turning around there certainly was a conversion: the persecutor was now a defender of what he had formerly attacked.[10]

1.16 *to reveal his Son in and through me*: REB thus gets round a difficulty. The Greek has 'to reveal his Son in me' and it is hard to be sure what that could mean. Why does Paul not say 'to reveal his Son to me'? The suspicion that something more inward is at stake is perhaps behind REB's rendering. Certainly in 2.20 Paul will speak of Christ as living in and through him, and it is possible that he is pointing forward to that. Grayston (p. 19) rather neatly suggests 'in my consciousness and in my life and work'.

1.17 *those who were apostles before me*: he must concede that their apostleship is older, but will not agree that it is greater in significance or standing. As elsewhere (e.g. I Cor. 9.1; 15.3–10) he sees himself as apostle in the same sense as Peter and the others (see on v. 1 above).

Arabia: a much wider area than modern Saudi-Arabia. To judge from II Cor. 11.32f., where Paul was in danger from the Nabataean king Aretas, it was in his territory centred on Petra that Paul spent this time. As Bruce points out, this makes it likely that Paul was doing more than praying and contemplating, he was carrying on some kind of mission. He would hardly fall foul of the authorities by passive contemplation. Yet if there was an Arabian mission, we are told nothing about it.

Damascus: this is the nearest Paul comes to telling us that his 'revelation' was on the road to Damascus (but see Acts 9.3). He says he *returned to Damascus*, implying that he had been there already (and see Acts 9.8).

1.18 *to get to know Cephas*: the name is the Aramaic equivalent of 'Peter', or as we might say 'Rock'. Paul uses the Aramaic form throughout the letter, except in 2.7–8, and in I Cor. 1.12 etc. No one really knows why, especially as he is not writing to Aramaic speakers. It is tempting to suppose that Paul associates him with a Jewish-Christian understanding of the gospel, and so uses his Jewish name, but that is only a guess.

Get to know renders *historēsai* which could also mean something like 'consult', 'make enquiries of'. However the particular grammatical way in which the word is used here makes that unlikely (see Fung p. 74). Moreover as Paul is minimizing his dependence on the Jerusalem authorities, REB is more likely to be right (see vv. 1, 11f.).

1.19 *none of the other apostles, except James*: this James was clearly a leading figure in the early Jerusalem church and had influence well beyond it (see Acts 12.17; 15.13; 21.18; I Cor. 15.7; Gal. 2.9, 12; James 1.1; Jude 1; see also the reference to him in Josephus, *Ant.* 20.200). Nevertheless it is not altogether certain that he was counted as an

apostle by all Christians; here and in I Cor. 15.7 it is possible to take
the wording either to include him as an apostle, or to exclude him. In
both cases it is a little easier grammatically to have him included. To
judge from his coolness to the mission of Jesus reported in John 7.5
and endorsed by Mark 3.31–35 and similar passages where the
brothers of Jesus are outside the circle of his friends and supporters,
the resurrection appearance of I Cor. 15.7 must have had a dramatic
effect on him.

1.22   *the Christian congregations*: literally 'the churches in Christ'.
Paul often uses the expression 'in Christ' and it is not at all easy to
determine its full meaning. *Christian* is not incorrect, but does not
bring out the full flavour: perhaps something like 'being under
Christ's lordship and living in his power' is implied.[11]

The meeting at Jerusalem
2.1–10

This is the second part of the narration section of the letter. In the first
part Paul has emphasized how few and brief were his contacts with
Jerusalem but has made it evident that there were no objections on
the part of the church there to what he was doing. Now he tells the
story of a momentous meeting in Jerusalem which is probably
intended to represent the same event as that of Acts 15, though the
identification cannot be certain (see Essay II). In any case, our task is
to understand the story as it is told here, and not to make com-
parisons with Acts 15 unless it is illuminating to do so. Why the
meeting took place is not obvious: Paul says he went to Jerusalem
because of *a revelation from God* (v. 2), but we are not told what that
was. Certainly he explains his gospel, or at least his distinctive
presentation of it, to important but unspecified Christian leaders
there. That the issue that had caused the problem was circumcision,
together with other Jewish legal requirements of Gentile converts,
emerges somewhat obliquely in v. 3 when we learn that *not even
Titus, Greek though he is, was compelled to be circumcised*. Even that is
ambiguous: it could mean that Titus was circumcised but not under
compulsion, or that he was not forced to be and was not. Yet it must
surely be the latter, for if Paul had consented to the circumcision of a
Greek he would have compromised his whole position and would

scarcely want to talk about it here. Those who had urged his *circumcision* (v. 4) had done so only to appease *certain sham Christians* who had *sneaked in* to the meeting to investigate reports about Paul, probably that he was imperilling the integrity of the people of God by admitting Gentiles who had not accepted their covenant obligations and had not even been circumcised. Paul regards as *bondage* what they wish to insist upon and says he rejected it as endangering *the full truth of the gospel* for the Gentiles, v. 5.

There is something a little strange about the passage that follows (v. 6). Paul says that *those of repute* (the same expression as in v. 2) made no further requirements of Paul, which is to say that he won his case: the Gentiles did not need to be circumcised in order to be within the people of God. The strange thing is that this reference to the important people in the Jerusalem church is accompanied by a more than slightly derogatory aside (*God does not recognize these personal distinctions*) as it is not in v. 2 or v. 9. Perhaps it is just that as Paul does not accept their authority over him, he does not want to let their repute go altogether unchallenged. There seem to be three groups of people at the meeting: Paul and his colleagues, then the Jerusalem Christian leaders, and then a third group who could be straightforwardly Jews not claiming to be Christians at all or Jewish Christians who wanted to Judaize all Gentile converts. According to Paul's account, despite the endeavours of the third group whoever they were, the second group (*those of repute*) accepted Paul's mission on his terms without qualification. If this is the same event as that described in Acts 15, it must be said that at this point the accounts disagree. In Acts the Gentiles are also obliged to accept certain important dietary restrictions (see Acts 15.20, 29; 16.4) together with some moral requirements, and Paul not only consents to this but helps to circulate the decree. There is nothing of this in Galatians.

From the Jewish point of view it was almost certainly not that the circumcision of the Gentiles was being regarded as essential for their salvation. Gentiles were commonly expected to be saved without circumcision and the full observance of the Torah, so long as they lived righteously as Gentiles. In practice this meant keeping the so-called Noachic commandments by avoiding injustice, incest, the dishonouring of parents, adultery and promiscuity, and by practising love of neighbour, see *Jub.* 7.20–21. Of course some Jews would not have regarded these as enough, but at least many would have accepted that Gentiles could be saved if they kept these commands.[12] What would not be at all easily accepted was the idea that such people could be fully within the covenant people of God, and it is for precisely this inclusion that Paul argues. Two options he does not even discuss: the first, that Jews are the true people of God and Gentile Christians are second-class members living on the fringe; the second, that there are two peoples of God, one Jewish and one Gentile Christian. That there can be only one people of God is a presupposition for Paul. That Gentile adult males should be circumcised he appears to assume is not feasible. Therefore he is left with the position that now, in the dawn of the new age (1.4), membership of the people of God is through faith in Jesus Christ and through that alone. Nothing else can be added as a requirement. That this may have implications for salvation will emerge later, but at this point we are discussing the strictly community question, who is in and who is out.

So (v. 7) Paul's Gentile mission is accepted as running parallel to but as distinct from *the mission to the Jews* which is presented as the special responsibility of *Peter* (v. 8 also). Both were seen as the work of God. Apparently the agreement was that they should be kept separate, which obviously could not work for very long, as Galatians itself is witness, not to mention the dispute at Antioch. In many places the missions could not be kept separate because the communities could not be kept separate: in many parts of the world Jews and Gentiles lived side by side, and we shall see (vv. 11–14) that Paul cannot countenance parallel and independent Christian communities in the same town. There may be different house churches but to use our terminology they must be in communion with one another. The agreement at Jerusalem was thus successful in that it gave Paul the endorsement he wanted (but denies he needed). It was unsuccessful in solving the problem of how Gentiles and observant Jews could live together in the same Christian community. Nevertheless the agreement is made solemnly binding (v. 9) and it is possible that it was even made legally binding. The handshake may represent the Roman *societas*, in effect a legally enforceable partnership between equals, with the obligation to remember *the poor* (the poor Christians in Jerusalem probably) as one of the clauses in the contract, perhaps the only clause other than the demarcation of areas itself.[13]

If the general outline of what happened is not easy to determine, many of the details are equally difficult to be sure about.

* * * *

2.1 *Fourteen years later*: this could be fourteen years after his call/ conversion, or fourteen years after the visit of 1.18. According to Paul, this is only his second visit to Jerusalem after his call, but if we identify it with that in Acts 15, then in 11.30 Acts has an extra visit which Paul does not mention. Yet he is solemnly setting out the sum total of his contacts with the Jerusalem church, and it is hard to believe he would wilfully or absent-mindedly omit one visit. See Essay II.

Barnabas: frequently mentioned in Acts as a companion of Paul, with whom he later had a disagreement (see especially Acts 13–15, and compare the causes of disagreement in Acts 15.39 and in v. 13 below; see also I Cor. 9.6 and Col. 4.10).

2.2 *a revelation from God*: those who think that the Gal.2 visit to Jerusalem was not that of Acts 15 but that of Acts 11.27–30, suggest that this revelation was the forecast of famine given through Agabus. See Essay II. In this letter Paul does not say what the revelation was nor what form it took.

the gospel which I preach to the Gentiles: the nearest this letter comes to defining the gospel is in 2.15–16 (see below). See also Rom. 1.16–17.

that the race I had run and was running should not be in vain: why should it be in vain, and why should he need Jerusalem to reassure him that it was not? He clearly does not believe that he needs their instruction (1.11–12) nor that his understanding of Christian truth is subject to their ratification. Perhaps he fears a schism in the Christian movement, perhaps he believes it is vital that his Gentile churches should be in communion with the mother church, or perhaps he is afraid now and had been afraid then that his converts may be tempted to defect to the law-gospel of his opponents, and then his work really will have been in vain. The last possibility seems the most likely: he was trying to ensure that the Jerusalem church did not lend its support to any who would subvert his mission.

2.4 *certain sham Christians*: literally 'false brethren', who may not have been Christians at all but may have been posing as sympathizers. On the other hand they may have been Jewish Christians who were more concerned with the Jewish than the Christian part of their allegiance, and in Paul's view were not true Christians.

to spy on the liberty we enjoy: why should they have objected so strongly to the liberty from Jewish legal requirements that Paul maintained for his converts? There are several possibilities.

15

(i) We may have here the beginnings of Jewish xenophobia in the run-up to the Jewish revolt from 66 onwards, when all fraternizing with the Gentile enemy was regarded as treasonable. Jewish Christians might well have felt vulnerable, especially in view of the Pauline Gentile mission, to charges from deeply patriotic Jews that they were of suspect loyalty.

(ii) The objections on the other hand may have been more religious than patriotic and may have arisen from fears that the nascent Christian movement would lead to disloyalty to the covenant and to the Torah.

(iii) If the *sham Christians* were not Jews but (Jewish) Christians, they may have wanted to ensure that the Christian movement stayed firmly within the fold of historical Israel, even if this meant requiring circumcision of male adult converts.

Unfortunately Paul does not explain their motives nor give clear identification of them. All we know is that he regarded their behaviour as underhand: they were *intruders who had sneaked in to spy*.

2.5 *that the full truth of the gospel should be maintained for you*: Paul still has not explained why accepting circumcision and its consequences should imperil the truth of the gospel. Later (2.21) he will argue that to do so would imply that Christ is not enough, and later still that this acceptance would be to say that the gospel was for Jews only (3.18).

REB has a footnote to this verse, indicating that some MSS omit *not* from the beginning of it. This would mean that Paul did briefly give way, but then thought better of it. The evidence of the MSS is strongly in support of the text as translated in REB, and it is possible that some copyists, chiefly in the West, omitted *not* in order to achieve harmony with Paul's principle of accommodation set out in I Cor. 9.20–23. Such a reading would run so contrary to Paul's whole argument in this passage that it must be regarded as very unlikely (see Metzger, pp. 591f).

2.6 *imparted nothing further to me*: this could mean either (i) that they did not find Paul's gospel incomplete nor thought it needed supplementing, or (ii) that they did not lay down any extra requirements on Paul's Gentile converts. The effect is much the same in either case.

2.7 *Peter*: only here and in v. 8 does Paul call him by this name. Elsewhere in the Pauline letters he is always Cephas, as in v. 11. It is just possible that the present deviation from the usual practice arises from Paul's using a report of the meeting, in which the name *Peter* was used. We notice that there is no hint of awareness of the Cornelius incident of Acts 10–11.

2.9   *James, Cephas, and John*: these must surely be *those of repute* of vv. 2.6. James and Cephas we have already met; John is presumably the disciple and one of the sons of Zebedee, Matt.4.21 etc.

pillars of the community: the metaphor goes back to the pillars of the Temple presumably, cf. I Kings 7.15 for example where the same word for *pillars* is used in LXX. For the same metaphor see Rev. 3.12; I Clem.5.2, and in IV Macc.17.3 the martyrs are the pillars of the world. The underlying and not uncommon idea is that the community functions like a sanctuary, see 1QS 8.1–6 (the Qumran Community Rule); I Cor. 3.16f.; II Cor. 6.16; Heb.3.6; 10.21; I Peter 2.5; Rev. 3.12.

2.10   *we should keep in mind the poor*: these could be poor people anywhere. It is nevertheless more likely that this is the initial impetus for Paul's collection of money for the poor Christians in Jerusalem, see Rom. 15.25–28; I Cor. 16.1–4; II Cor. 8.1–9.15, which came to loom so large on his horizon. This could have been simply an early form of Christian Aid, but it is also possible that here *poor* has the connotation of the pious, Godfearing people as it often does in Jewish writing, e.g. Prov. 19.22; *Pss.Sol.*5.2; 10.6; 1QM 11; 1QH 2, 3; 1QpHab 12. In any case, one reason for the collection was obviously financial need, but other reasons doubtless operated, including the fostering of the unity of the various Christian churches.

The Antioch incident
2.11–14

As the third part of the narration, Paul now presents to the Galatians what amounts to a parallel case to their own situation, expecting them to overhear the Antioch debate and wear the cap where it fits.[14] Almost certainly Paul is working in chronological sequence. Though this is sometimes questioned, the way in which he sets out the stories virtually in steps makes it probable that the Antioch affair was subsequent to, and perhaps not very long after, the agreement made in Jerusalem (2.1–10). The present order of events also makes good logical sense, as we shall see. If the Jerusalem meeting was, in Paul's mind at least, held to settle the question whether Gentiles needed to be circumcised in order to be fully within the one people of God, the dispute at Antioch was initially about whether Jews should continue to observe the normal rules of the covenant people, and in particular the food laws. Yet the latter issue has implications for the former: if Jewish Christians cannot have full table fellowship with Gentile Christians, then we are back with two groups of Christians who are not in full communion with one another, in effect with two parallel peoples of God. This might then lead to the feeling that the observant Jewish Christian group was more fully God's people than was the non-observant Gentile Christian group. Therefore, while in principle Paul may have no objection to Jewish Christians' maintaining their ancestral Torah-observance in matters of diet, see I Cor. 9.20 and perhaps Rom. 14, in practice he believes that such practice may have to be sacrificed if it stands in the way of table fellowship with Gentile Christians. The only other way out would be for Gentile converts to be obliged to keep the food laws, which for Paul runs into the same objections as does circumcision.

There has been much debate about exactly what had been going on in Antioch, about why it was found objectionable by the *messengers from James*, about why Peter then *drew back* and from what (v. 12).[15] The story is undeniably obscure, and the explanation offered here is probably the simplest but by no means the uncontested explanation. We suggest, then, that Peter at Antioch was sharing table fellowship with Gentile Christians, probably in their houses and therefore on their terms, i.e. without being sure that the food offered was in accordance with the food laws that were binding on Jews but not on Gentiles. Perhaps it was, perhaps it was not, but it looks as if no one minded much either way. There should have been no problem if Gentiles had eaten in observant Jewish houses, for it was not normal Jewish practice to avoid table fellowship with Gentiles when it was in Jewish houses and on Jewish terms, nor was there anything in the Torah to forbid it. It is true that some ultra-strict Jews avoided as far as possible any contact with Gentiles, but these would be unlikely to be Christians and equally unlikely to expect a community well away from Palestine to be able to or to want to maintain such separation.[16] It is likely, therefore, that Peter and the others were doing in effect what Paul recommended in I Cor. 9.20–21, not bothering about the food laws when in Gentile company in Gentile houses. There was no possibility of neutral ground: the first Christians had to meet in someone's house, and it is reasonable to suppose that in Antioch they were meeting in Gentile houses. This reconstruction means that what was objected to when the *messengers came from James* – presumably as representing the Jerusalem church – was that Peter and the others were not maintaining Jewish practice. To admit Gentiles to the church without requiring circumcision was one thing, and they had accepted that, but to consent to Jewish Christian abandonment of the dietary laws was quite another thing and they could not accept it.

So then, in the light of such objections, Peter, *Barnabas* and *the other Jewish Christians* (v. 13) *drew back and began to hold aloof* (v. 12). Paul, however, seems to imply that this is to go back on the Jerusalem agreement (v. 11) and certainly sees it as compromising *the truth of the gospel*, v. 14. He does not spell out why it has this implication, but surely it must have been because if Peter and the others are right, then Gentile Christians must obey the dietary laws if table fellowship is to continue. This is not in itself to require their circumcision, but it is a parallel case. In both cases it is a matter of whether it is necessary to be a Jew in order to be a Christian. Paul is convinced it is not.

All this is certainly to read to some extent between the lines, but some such reading is essential if we are to make sense of the story. Paul's rebuke to Peter is quite straightforward: if you were prepared *to live* (eat) *like a Gentile* (v. 14), how can you now require Gentiles to do what you yourself were until very recently prepared to forgo, namely observe the food laws? We have already mentioned Paul's principle of accommodation in I Cor. 9.20–21, living as a Jew when with Jews and as a Gentile when with Gentiles. The trouble with this clearly emerges in the Antioch affair: the two groups cannot be kept apart. It was a middle position that was inherently unstable. What happens when one has to live with Jews and with Gentiles in the same place? Once the people from Jerusalem had arrived, that was the problem. In the end, as we all know, the great mass of Christendom simply by-passed such questions and in practice became completely Gentile, though observant Jewish Christianity did continue in some places for a considerable time.[17]

* * * *

2.11   *Antioch*: a large cosmopolitan centre in what was then Syria and is now Turkey, modern Antakya, with a considerable Jewish community. It became one of the major centres of early Christianity.

2.12   *he was taking his meals with Gentile Christians*: the wording of REB tends to support the position adopted above, namely that he was eating with them, not they with him. Some infringements of Jewish food laws, such as eating pork, would be obvious, but others would not, and perhaps the essential point is that one could never be sure. The Greek is literally 'he was in the habit of eating ...' so that a regular practice is implied. It is not clear whether we are talking about ordinary meals, or the eucharist (perhaps in the context of an ordinary meal).

he was afraid of the Jews: Jews might have objected for political/nationalistic reasons, or for strictly religious reasons, or quite possibly both, though it is hard to believe religious reasons were absent.

2.13   *the same lack of principle*: the Greek word *hypokrisis* is often translated 'hypocrisy' but that does not suit the present context. The meaning could be as in REB, i.e. a mismatch between profession and action, or it could more simply be defiance of God, i.e. a standing against the truth. Either meaning is possible here.[18]

the truth of the gospel: Paul's objection to the conduct of Barnahas and the others is not just that it fractured the Christian fellowship of Antioch, but that it was inconsistent with the gospel as he saw it. Behind the community question lies a theological question: what is it that qualifies men and women, Jew and Gentile, for membership of God's people and acceptability with him? Almost immediately Paul will give in answer his basic principle that it is faith in Jesus Christ and that alone. Implicitly Peter and Barnabas and the rest were conceding that such faith is not enough, and that meeting certain requirements of the Torah is also needed. Although the issue here is not directly circumcision, the principle is the same: are Jesus Christ and faith in him enough, or are they not?

live like a Gentile and not like a Jew: the three great 'identity markers'[19] for Judaism were circumcision, observance of the Sabbath, and the dietary laws. Particularly in social terms, it was these that marked the difference between living Jewishly and living like the Gentiles. Here it is the last of these that is the centre of the controversy.

The fundamental proposition
2.15–21

At long last we come to the heart of Paul's contention in this letter. It is not without its difficulties which are discussed in the detailed notes, but what is offered here is one possible account of the argument. Presumably the rebuke to Peter delivered at Antioch has ended, and Paul now draws his conclusions for his Galatian readers/hearers. *We ourselves* (v. 15) presumably refers to Paul himself and Jewish Christians like him who have been brought up within the covenant people, as Gentiles have not (*sinners* could reflect a common Jewish view that Gentiles tended to be incorrigibly sinful in a general moral sense, cf. Rom. 1.18–32, or it could be less condemnatory in moral terms and reflect the fact that Gentiles do not have the Torah and so do not follow the full will of God). Yet it is precisely people like Paul who have come to recognize that men and women are accepted by God into his people (*justified*) not by observance of the Torah but by *faith in Christ Jesus* and by that alone. So he and Jews like him have turned to faith in Christ in order to find justification (v. 16), knowing that such acceptance by God can never be found through Torah-observance. It can be argued that Paul is here talking only about entry into God's people, not about the consequent life as that people, yet it seems impossible to maintain such a distinction.[20] The language he uses seems more general than that, and in any case the issue arises out of the Antioch incident which is primarily about how people who already consider themselves God's people ought to live. Paul's answer is that it is faith in Jesus Christ that both enables them to enter and also enables them to remain as his people, acceptable to him.

If Jews who turn to Christ then fail to be fully Torah-observant and so become strictly speaking *sinners* like *the Gentiles* (v. 17) this does not mean that Christ promotes sin. Indeed not (v. 18): it rather shows that the definition of sin is wrong. The real sin would be to reassert those distinctions between Jews and Gentiles (the 'identity markers') found in the law, or perhaps to re-assert that it is not faith in Jesus Christ that is the sole and sufficient ground of acceptance with God but that Torah-observance is necessary as well or instead. That would be the real infringement of God's will (make Paul *one who breaks the law*, v. 18: but it is important to note that in the Greek the word *law* does not occur, and we may take it that the infringement would be of God's will in general and not the law in particular).

Paul has elsewhere (Rom. 7.1–6) spoken of Christians as those who have *died to law*, v. 19. The point seems to be that the law is here seen as a regime which is no longer Paul's final authority, and in that sense he has *died* to it. The basic idea is not uncommon in Paul. Now that his life is centred in Christ and lived under the authority and in the power of Christ and his Spirit (e.g. Rom. 8.1–17) he is freed from all other powers and authorities, see Rom. 8.2, 4, 9, 37f. In effect, no one can serve two masters, and if Christ is the master now, then nothing else and nobody else can be. If the basic idea is not unusual, what is unusual here is that he says that it was *through the law* that he died to the law: what does this mean? One could argue that there is a reflection of the notion of dying with Christ, cf. v. 20 and Rom. 6.1–11; Col. 2.20; 3.3. Now Christ died to the law (escaped from its power) when he underwent the curse of the law (3.13) and came out unscathed. Those who die with Christ thus die through the law. This interpretation is not altogether satisfactory, if only because the law did not bring about the death of Christ: it was subsequent to his death that he underwent the curse of the law (see below on 3.13). Yet if we do not press the details of the text too hard, it could be possible to say that Christ died *through the law* and so Paul with him: that interpretation does at least depend on material in Galatians itself.

It may be easier, however, to detect a hint of Pauline autobiography here, reflecting what is implicit in 1.13–16: it was through his fanatical adherence to the law that Paul himself was brought to persecuting the nascent Christian community, but was then converted, literally turned round, so that he joined the very people whom he had persecuted. In a sense then, it was *through the law* (i.e. through his zealous devotion to the law) that he came to meet Christ and then *died to the law*. Paradoxically, since as a Jew he had believed that keeping the law was living for God, it was when he died to the law that he came *to live for God*. How the law can be both God-given and also something to which to die, he will take up later in the letter, see especially 3.19–25.

In any case, his old life came to an end and he was *crucified with*

Christ: not literally of course, but in so far as he was released from his old securities and goals and above all from the old authorities and powers under which he had lived. We are dealing with something close to a change of identity, and certainly a change of social identity.[21] His present life is firmly centred in Christ (v. 20) and in faith in him *who loved* him *and gave himself for* him. Once again a reference to the death of Christ for others is left unexplained (cf. 1.4), but in the light of the beginning of the verse, *I have been crucified with Christ*, that death can be understood as enabling others to die with him, cf. II Cor. 5.14–15. It was not to replace their deaths, but to bring them about, their deaths to all the old powers and authorities. Because all this is central for Paul, any attempt to supplement it or to replace it is tantamount to trying to *nullify the grace of God*. No doubt Paul's opponents would have hotly denied that they were imperilling the grace of God, which was after all at the heart of Judaism. For Paul, however, that grace of God is to be found definitively in Jesus Christ and in his death, and to insist on Torah-observance as part of the life of God's people (*righteousness*, v. 21), as implicitly happened at Antioch, is to derogate from or even to nullify that grace. In the end, if Torah-observance is still essential then we do not need Christ, who thus *died for nothing*.

* * * *

2.16 *but only through faith in Jesus Christ*: as REB has the verse, and as we have assumed above, Paul is saying that even born Jews know (if they are also Christians) that it is not keeping the law that makes people acceptable to God and members of his people, but rather faith in Christ. The two ways are alternatives, but only one gets to the destination. It can be argued, however[22] that here Paul first states the Jewish Christian position, which is that doing the law needs to be accompanied by faith in Christ. The verse then runs:

> 'We Christian Jews, who are not sinful Gentiles, know that doing the works of the law does not place people within the covenant community, unless there is also faith in Christ Jesus'

– or something like that at any rate. On this argument, the second part of the verse is where Paul moves beyond this Jewish Christian position and proposes faith in Christ not as a complement to Torah-

23

observance but as an alternative to it, so that we are *justified by this faith and not through actions dictated by law*. In this interpretation, the Greek *ean mē* is given its usual meaning 'unless' rather than *but only* as in REB. The difficulty with this whole proposal is that it has Paul making a significant argumentative move in the middle of the verse from the Jewish Christian normal position to his own, without making the shift even half clear. Therefore while this proposal cannot be brushed aside, it nevertheless appears less probable than the usual understanding of the argument at this point, that implied by REB, namely that both halves of the verse say much the same thing, that even Jews like Paul know that justification is through faith in Christ and not by keeping the law.

faith in Jesus Christ: there are two interlocking questions here, the meaning of *faith* (Greek *pistis*) and whether we should read 'faith *in* Jesus Christ' or 'the faith(fulness) *of* Jesus Christ'.

(i) *Pistis* has a range of meanings which includes something like 'the faith' in the sense of the Christian faith, which may perhaps be reflected in 1.23, faithfulness, belief, and the sort of response which combines reliance and commitment. It is the last that is usually regarded as characteristically Pauline, especially where justification is being spoken of, and it is certainly present in the next part of the present verse, *we too have put our faith in Jesus Christ*. It is essentially the human acceptance of the unconditional offer of God. This is the interpretation implied by REB.

(ii) If however we take the Greek literally it could run differently, because the *pistis* of Jesus Christ is surely not his faith in the sense of (i) just outlined, but his faithfulness (to his Father's will, presumably, cf. Rom. 5.19 for example). It is increasingly argued that here and in 3.22 and in some other places we ought to take the genitive at its face value to mean 'of' not 'in'.[23] If this is right, then the line of thought in this verse is that we are justified first by the faithful action of Jesus Christ in undergoing the cross (presumably) and then by our response to, our faith in, that faithful action. This way of taking the phrase is gaining ground in scholarly circles and certainly makes good sense, but it cannot be said that the issue is settled.

justified: this is the first occurrence of the verb (Greek *dikaioō*) that is so important in Galatians. It is common in LXX, where it usually means something like 'vindicate, prove/find to be in the right', but where it also often denotes restoration to proper relationship with God and with other people within the covenant with God. There is often but not always a forensic colouring, where the implied setting is a court of law at which someone receives justice. In Paul it normally denotes the giving of a right standing within God's people and with God, a standing that may very well be undeserved because it is the result of God's unconditional generosity (grace). It is thus virtually the same as acceptance and has both a Godward and a community reference, as it clearly does here: throughout this chapter the community issue (who can have fellowship with whom) runs into the issue of acceptability before God. It is probably also impossible to confine the term to entry into God's people or his favour; it is indeed primarily an entry term, but as the present passage is concerned with the conditions of being God's people as much as with the conditions of entry into that people, it is hard to confine it to the latter. Moreover in all probability it has a future dimension, and can be used of God's verdict at the Judgment: compare 3.6 with 5.5, and Rom. 3.24, 26, 28; 4.2–12; 5.1, 9; 6.7; 8.30 REB with Rom. 2.13; 3.30.[24]

doing what the law requires . . . actions dictated by law . . . keeping the law: all these expressions in REB translate the same Greek words, literally 'works of law'. It has usually been assumed that Paul was writing quite generally about all or any of the commands of the Torah. It has now been argued, however, that this term refers specifically to the three great 'identity markers' of the Jewish community, namely circumcision, the Sabbath and the dietary laws, and that Paul is simply not talking about the law in general. His concern is strictly with those matters in the law that serve to demarcate Jews from Gentiles, and we consequently ought not to enlarge his focus to the law as a whole.[25]

Now it is true that in this letter the matters from the law with which Paul is particularly concerned are circumcision (2.3; 5.2, 3, 6, 11; 6.12–13, 15) and dietary laws (2.11–14). There is no mention of the Sabbath. The only other specific point from the law that is quoted is the command to love, 5.14. It is true also, as both the account of the Jerusalem meeting and the story of the Antioch affair show, that what marks out a community from another or from its surrounding society was at the heart of Paul's dispute with his opponents. On the other hand, most of Paul's argument is about the law without qualification or restriction (e.g. 2.19, 21; 3.11, 12, 19, 21, 23, 24; 4.21; 5.4 etc.) and although he does attack in the first instance both circumcision and the food laws as requirements of the people of God, the way in which he mounts his attack is to relegate the importance of the law as such, not just three important items within it. We may therefore agree that two of the identity markers are what spark off the debate behind this letter, but need not go on to accept that the focus is on them throughout the argument. They are the specific cases which lead to the general question and it is the general question which finally dominates Galatians. In any case, whether we take 'works of the law' to be any works of the law, or specifically circumcision, the Sabbath and the food laws, for Paul it is none of them that is necessary to constitute the people of God; rather what is needed is faith in Christ, acceptance by him and thereafter of him.

It is important to underline that in any case Paul is not here contrasting faith with morality or with good deeds. He is certainly being more particular than that, and is contrasting a community that is based only on faith in Christ with one that is based on living Jewishly (v. 14).

no human being can be justified by keeping the law: see Ps. 143.2. Paul does not say that it is impossible to keep the law, but rather that this is not the way to find justification. Did anyone think it was? It is obvious, for example, from the book of Deuteronomy that for Israel it was God's grace in election that made her his people, and that their observance of the Torah was people's grateful response, their way of living within the covenant which he had generously given them (see for example Deut. 10.12–11.32). Judaism did not and does not teach that law-observance is what constitutes Israel as God's people, though of course it did and does teach that such observance is the way of living as his people. Yet here Paul finds it necessary to deny what presumably no instructed Jew would ever have found it necessary to affirm, viz. that justification is by works of the law, however these are defined. Why? There are several possibilities.

(i) The people whom Paul was opposing did not represent mainstream Judaism but a somewhat distorted form of it, a merit-centred form which is indeed found after CE 70, for example in II(4) Esd.9.7 and *II Apoc.Bar*. 14.7,12. While this possibility cannot be ruled out, there is no contemporary evidence for it.

(ii) Paul's opponents did not themselves have a very instructed understanding of Judaism and were quite unaware that law-observance was how to live as God's people but was not a condition of entry. This would be parallel to their supposed unawareness that circumcision was no isolated matter but carried with it the obligation to keep the whole Torah, 5.3. Perhaps innocently but ignorantly they were simply arguing that circumcision was the condition of being acceptable to God.

(iii) The most feasible suggestion is that Paul is not attacking a position that anyone consciously holds, but is rather exposing the logic of those who are insisting on circumcision and other matters. In effect he is saying, if you require circumcision and observance of the dietary laws (with or without the rest of the Torah) as well as faith in Jesus Christ for entry into God's people, then you are saying that the law is necessary for justification.

It is worth noting that *can be justified* is in Greek in the future tense. This may indicate that Paul is talking about God's acceptance at the Last Judgment, though as it comes in a quotation from LXX we cannot be sure.

2.17 *justified in Christ*: the expression is unusual. Perhaps the preposition *in* simply means 'by' which is possible in NT Greek. Perhaps however *in Christ* has something of its frequent force in Paul's writings and indicates that it is in the sphere of Christ's power that people are justified, cf. above on 1.22.

we no less than the Gentiles turn out to be sinners: the interpretation we have adopted above is that *sinners* is not to be understood in ordinary moral terms but as 'not fully Torah-observant'. Today, with our resources of punctuation, we should doubtless put *sinners* in inverted commas.

does that mean that Christ is a promoter of sin? Of course not! the last three words translate *mē genoito*, an extremely emphatic denial. We should perhaps say something like 'not on your life' because the conclusion is ridiculous. It is so ridiculous that something must be wrong with the premises that have led to it, and what is wrong is the definition of sin. Gentile Christians who are not law-observant are not thereby sinners, nor are Jewish Christians like Paul himself who are prepared to forgo certain observances in order to maintain one fellowship within the church.

2.18 *On the contrary…*: the real sin is not to sit loose to things like circumcision and dietary laws (as Paul's opponents presumably think). The real sin would rather be to start insisting all over again on law-observance as a condition of being in God's people, for that would amount to saying that Christ and faith in him were not enough. It would also be to re-assert the division between Jew and Gentile. The point is that for Paul the distinction between sinner and righteous is no longer determined simply by the Torah.

It is worth noting that at this verse Paul switches from 'we' to *I*. It is likely that this is purely rhetorical, but it is conceivable that the change is significant and that he is saying something like 'if I in my ministry were to start insisting on certain law-observances . . .' *then I prove to be one that breaks the law*: we noted above that the word for *law* (*nomos*) does not occur in the Greek, though it may be held that what one *breaks* (literally 'be a transgressor') must be that.

If that is correct, and if REB is thus correct, the meaning is: 'if we bring back the law, and especially things like the food laws, then judged by that standard I am indeed a law-breaker.' The view adopted in the main comment above, however, is that what Paul would break would be not the law but the more fundamental will of God if he were to reassert such things. We have adopted it because it seems to suit the drift of the passage better.

2.19   *through the law I died to the law*: we suggested above alternative ways of explaining *through the law*, but in fact there are several possibilities.

(i) There is a reference to Paul's own life, where his zeal for the law led him, by way of persecuting Christians, to his encounter with Christ and so to his dying to the law (the view we preferred).

(ii) There is an implied reference to dying with Christ who died to the curse of the law (3.13) (a view we found possible, even though it does not fit the text very comfortably).

(iii) Because the demands of the law made it scarcely feasible for Gentiles to become Christians other than through Paul's law-free gospel, Paul found it necessary to die to the law.

(iv) The law in its wider sense as the Pentateuch and not just the laws within it, leads to dying to the law: this is to anticipate the argument of 3.6ff. and its quotation of Gen. 15.6 in favour of faith as sufficient for entry into the people of God (and the progeny of Abraham). This would be a stronger candidate if we did not have to anticipate something uncomfortably far ahead in the letter. It must be conceded that this sort of anticipation is not impossible, however, in a letter which does not disclose the basic issue until quite late in its course.

(v) The law showed the need for redemption by giving awareness of sin: this is one way of taking 3.19–25. The law itself thus showed that I needed to die to sin perhaps, but did it show that I needed to die to the law?

None of these explanations is altogether impossible, and none appears inescapably correct. The verse remains problematic.

to live for God: REB slightly obscures the parallelism in the Greek, which more literally could be translated 'I died to law in order to live to God'. The datives seem to represent alternative powers or regimes.[26] What is remarkable here is that instead of seeing the law as representing the regime or power of God Paul sees it as an alternative, which incidentally supports the interpretation we have adopted for v. 18.

2.20 *I have been crucified with Christ*: for the same idea see 5.24; 6.14 and Rom. 6.1–11. At least for Paul, the old world is now over (see 1.4) and his present life is for God, v. 19. In the classic passage on dying with Christ (Rom. 6) there is an explicit link with baptism and also with resurrection. Neither note is sounded here and ought not to be imported into the passage, though see immediately below.

the life I now live is not my life, but the life which Christ lives in me: taken literally, this is of course an exaggeration. His life in the obvious sense is still his life. Yet in terms of its centre and its governance it is not his, for it is centred in Christ (and in his Spirit, see chapter 5) and is under Christ's lordship. We ought not to take this clearly rhetorical way of putting things as a philosophical denial of the existence of the self.

It is comparatively rare to find in Paul's writings the notion of Christ in us, whereas the notion of our being in Christ is very common. The suggestion is probably correct that while the more frequent reference to believers' being in Christ concerns the basis of their existence, Christ's being in the believers is more a matter of his acting in and through them.[27] If so, REB's rendering here is appropriate (the Greek is more literally 'I live and yet not I, but Christ lives in me'). The expression refers to the basic springs of action, and thus fits well in a context concerned with how one defines sin: it is not law, but Christ's activity within them which makes believers righteous and which therefore distinguishes them from sinners. What sort of life this turns out to be will be dealt with in chapters 4 and 5, but the connection of *life* with *Christ* certainly suggests an allusion to the resurrection.

I here is almost certainly not particularly autobiographical but rather rhetorical, as in v. 18. All believers are in view, though naturally Paul himself is included.

my present mortal life: more literally, 'the life I now live in the flesh'. It is unlikely that 'flesh' (*sarx*) here means life without God as it does in chapter 5. REB's rendering is therefore perfectly appropriate, cf. II

Cor. 10.3. Nevertheless there may be overtones of human weakness as REB's *mortal* brings out. Betz on this expression plausibly suggests that Paul is emphasizing that Christian life is lived under normal human conditions and that having Christ in us does not mean that we are in some way translated out of ordinary humanity or ordinary circumstances.

   the Son of God: cf. 1.16. There is a rich literature on the meaning of this designation of Christ.[28] The expression must not be confused with the later definition of him as 'God the Son', the Second Person of the Trinity. In the Bible a king can be called God's son, as can the people of Israel as a whole, and in Hellenistic Judaism the angels and the righteous (see for example, in order: II Sam. 7.14; Ex. 4.22; Deut. 32.43 LXX; Wisd. 5.5). In the NT Jesus is frequently called Son of God, e.g. Mark 1.1; Matt. 11.27; Acts 13.33; I Thess. 1.10; Rom. 8.3–4, 29; Gal. 4.5. The basic notion is of someone appointed, sent and commissioned by God, responsible and obedient to him. We too easily think of sonship in nearly sentimental terms, forgetting that one of the essential characteristics of true sons was – in biblical times and in many other societies – their obedience to their fathers. As God's Son, Jesus Christ is therefore not only the one who enjoys a special relationship with him but also the one who carries out his will. The same applies to the sonship of those who belong to the Son, see 4.1–7.

2.21   *if righteousness comes by law*: although *righteousness* (*dikaiosynē*) is more often than not here taken to mean 'justification' and thus to denote entry into God's people, it is perfectly feasible to let it have its usual meaning, 'living as God's people'. Both renderings make sense in the context but it is preferable to adopt the latter. Thus Paul is using the word here in its normal sense to denote how people live, and is perhaps reflecting the issue at Antioch which was primarily not about how one enters the people of God but about how one lives within it.[29] For Paul it is not only admission to that people but also remaining within it that is based on faith in Jesus Christ rather than on Torah-obedience.

First argument, from the Galatians' experience
3.1–5

Paul's vehemence is obvious, and leads him to be less than polite to the *Galatians*. He says that they are *stupid*, v. 1. They have listened to a graphic presentation of Christ crucified in preaching (presumably Paul's) and they have responded to it. As a result (v. 2) they received *the Spirit*, a sign that they were God's people of the New Age.[30] They therefore already have the clearest of indications that they are within that people, so why do they now propose to accept Jewish legal observances? Is the gift of the Spirit not enough for them? Having begun (v. 3) *with the spiritual*, that is with God's own power and therefore with his validation, do they now intend to revert to something lesser, *the material*, in the hope that this will make them complete (*perfect*)? *Material* is literally 'the flesh' and is surely a reference to circumcision, sometimes called 'the covenant in the flesh', see Gen. 17.13 and Ecclus. 44.20. At the same time it cannot be accidental that Paul here, as in chapter 5, juxtaposes and contrasts 'flesh' (*sarx*) and 'Spirit' (*Pneuma*); this opposition in Paul regularly signifies the contrast not between physical and non-physical, but between what is essentially God-centred and God-empowered and what is merely human.[31] It is true that usually *sarx* refers to things that are unambiguously bad (e.g. 5.13–21) as circumcision is not (6.15), so it is the more striking that he can use it here of something which traditionally stood for acceptance into the covenant and the covenant people. The point is that now that Christ and his Spirit have come and now that both Jews and Gentiles can be admitted into God's people by faith in Christ, to revert to the requirement of circumcision and what follows from it is to revert to the purely human after enjoying the God-given. This is strong language indeed and must have been found offensive by those who believed that circumcision itself was God-given. In Paul's defence it must be recognized that he is writing in the heat of controversy and it is important that in 6.16 he treats circumcision as irrelevant rather than as reprehensible. Nevertheless he says what he says: in moving from the gift of the Spirit on to an insistence on legal requirements they are not moving on towards completion or perfection. On the contrary they are moving backwards from the divine to the human. We have noted that this is not his last word on the subject, and we should bear in mind that later he will argue (3.23–25) that the law was God's temporary expedient which has had its day now that Christ has come.

Their own experience (v. 4) should surely be enough to show them how unnecessary it is now to turn to the law. They must be aware (v. 5) that already *God* has given them *the Spirit* and *works miracles among them* (he does not specify what these are): what more can they want? All that they presently enjoy came to them not at all from legal observance but entirely from their response (*faith*) to *the gospel message*. Their own shared experience ought to be sufficient to demonstrate to them that it is utterly redundant and wrong to talk of anything supplementary to Christ and faith in him.

* * * *

3.1 *You must have been bewitched*: strictly speaking this is a question, 'Who has bewitched you?' Paul in fact knows quite well, even if not precisely, who has led them astray. The use of the word 'bewitch' nicely suggests that they are scarcely responsible for their actions, and is congruent with his calling them *stupid*.

Jesus Christ was openly displayed on the cross: the imagery is strongly visual, yet the display must have been verbal, through the preaching (cf. v. 2, *the gospel message*). The point may be simply that it was like a public proclamation or placard, or more particularly that the preaching was pictorial and vivid. Paul does elsewhere say that his preaching was strongly cross-centred, e.g. I Cor. 1.23; 2.2; 15.3.

3.2 *did you receive the Spirit*: this is the first of the many mentions of the Spirit in this letter. It is significant that the reception of the Spirit is the point from which Paul argues, an agreed premise that apparently the Galatians themselves must accept. For a very striking statement of the belief that the Spirit will be given specifically to Israel and specifically in the Last Days (cf. Gal. 1.4) see Ezek. 36.22–27. For Paul, the indisputable fact that they have the Spirit is proof that they are God's people and his argument is that the law had nothing to do with it. It therefore cannot be a necessary condition for being the people of God.

Polemics apart, it is important to observe that for Paul the Spirit is the foundation of all Christian existence, not something added at a subsequent stage. See also 4.6, 29; 5.5, 16–25; 6.1, 8 and in other letters see, for example, Rom. 8.4–17; I Cor. 12.3.

by believing the gospel message: the Greek is more than a little ambiguous at this point. There are two words (*akoēs pisteōs*) which could be taken in a number of ways of which the only two serious options are 'hearing with faith' and *believing the gospel message*. Both make acceptable sense and either is defensible in this context.[32]

3.3 *Can you really be so stupid*: cf. v. 1. The point is surely not that they are showing themselves to be unintelligent exactly, but that they are showing a lack of discernment at a point that as Paul sees things is critical for true Christianity.

3.4 *all you have experienced*: the Greek (*epathete*) is ambiguous. We could translate either as REB, or 'all you have suffered'. If we follow REB there is a likely reference to the experience of the Spirit: is all that in vain (see v. 2)? If we translate 'suffered' there must be the implication of some form of persecution, but unless we count 4.29, which may reflect a measure of pressure by Jews on Gentile Christians, Galatians has no other mention of any persecution. As 4.29 is hardly sufficient to make us think that the Galatians were to any extent under persecution, and as the present context is concerned with the experience of the Spirit, REB is very probably right.
surely not: this seems to imply that the position is not irretrievable. Paul does not yet despair of persuading the Galatians out of their folly and cannot believe that their experience really will *come to nothing*.

3.5 *works miracles among you*: we have noticed that he does not say what these were. Paul does not often talk about miracle-working, but see Rom. 15.19; I Cor. 12.10, 28–29. However lightly stressed, they were undoubtedly seen by him as signs of the activity of the Spirit.
because you have faith in the gospel message: see the comment at v. 2, for this is the same expression. Paul sees things in sharp contrasts: when the Galatians responded to the gospel message (i.e. came to faith) they received the Spirit; therefore Torah-observance is not necessary. His opponents doubtless saw things differently: they need not have denied the reality of the Gentile Christians' experience, but would have argued that to be truly and fully members of God's people they ought to conform at least to basic Torah-

requirements. They saw as complementary what Paul saw as alternatives. For them one needed the Spirit *and* the Torah, but for Paul it was either/or.

Second argument, from Scripture (Abraham)
3.6–14

Paul now turns to the Torah itself, not to its commands but to one of its stories, that of Abraham. Abraham is crucial to Paul's presentation of the gospel without requiring the observance of all the laws of the Torah, not least because Jews universally regarded him as their father. He was the first to receive circumcision and the one from whom all Jews believed themselves to be descended in religious as well as in genealogical terms. The fact that both here and in Romans 4 Paul concentrates so heavily on Abraham may suggest that his opponents customarily made much use of his example.[33] In effect, 'Abraham is the father of the people of God, and if you Gentiles wish to be within that people you must not only have faith in Christ but also follow the example of Abraham and accept circumcision and what is implied in it, the observance of the will of God as conveyed by the Torah. If it was good enough for Abraham it is certainly good enough for you.'

This argument Paul faces head on. In brief his case is that the true progeny of Abraham are not those who are racially descended from him nor those who are circumcised, but those who share his faith. This means that Gentiles can as easily be his children as can Jews. The fact that Abraham was circumcised is not even mentioned (though it is in Rom. 4) nor is his willingness to sacrifice Isaac his son. The concentration is solely on Gen. 15.1–6. Abraham expects to die childless, but God assures him that he will have as many descendants as there are stars in the sky. Against all the odds, Abraham *put his faith in* (believed) *God, and that faith was counted to him as righteousness.* This is almost all that Paul cites from the story at this point, almost but not quite. He also quotes Gen. 12.3, '*In you all nations shall find blessing*' an addition that is important if he is to show that Abraham is as much the father of the non-Torah-keeping Gentiles as of the observant Jews.

It is hard to avoid the suspicion that in the background is the common picture of Abraham as the supremely righteous man, who even kept the Torah before it had been given, by anticipation as it were.[34] Moreover Abraham's readiness to sacrifice Isaac, his beloved and only freeborn son, out of his devotion to and trust in God (Gen. 22) was widely seen as the archetypal sacrifice, even though in the event it did not happen.[35] In contrast to all this Paul's interest is strictly in the faith of Abraham, the faith that counts as righteousness before God and which leads to the promise not only of innumerable descendants but also of the outflow of his blessing to the Gentiles (*all nations*). Paul thus achieves through the figure of Abraham both a primary emphasis on faith as what constitutes the people of God on the human side, and an emphasis on universality that embraces Jews and Gentiles equally. To his opponents therefore Paul in effect replies, 'If faith and faith alone was good enough for Abraham, it certainly ought to be good enough for the Gentiles.'

Now Abraham did not believe in Jesus Christ and Paul does not claim that he did. Yet in some way Abraham's faith in God's promise of progeny is fused with, or identified with, or made the archetype of, the faith in Jesus Christ of Gentile and Jew alike, though it is not just that. Abraham's faith is not just a symbol of Christian faith nor just a parallel case. It is crucial for Paul that it was precisely the father of the Jewish nation who acted thus and was treated by God thus (we must not forget that chapter 2 shows us that the issue is who constitutes the people of God and under what conditions). From the fact that Paul uses this argument twice, here and at more length in Rom. 4, it is evident that he lays great store upon it. What is more, he says (v. 9) that it is essential to have faith, which for him now means faith in Jesus Christ, to be children of Abraham and so share God's blessing on him.

In all this it is important to note that Paul separates and contrasts faith and Torah-obedience, as Judaism certainly did not. For most Jews, Abraham's faith (or faithfulness) was entirely congruent with his obedience to God understood in covenant-keeping and Torah-keeping terms. Once again he turns a both/and into an either/or. For him, it is because Abraham's faith is *only* his reliance on God's promise that he can be the prototype of the Gentile Christian.[36]

Up to this point in the section the key word has been *blessing*. He now (v. 10) contrasts this with *curse*, and argues that the opposite of relying solely on God's promise which leads to blessing like that on Abraham is relying on works of the law which leads to curse. Paul quotes Deut. 27.26 to show this. There is something strange about his use of this passage, in the first place because it says that if people fail to do what the law prescribes they are cursed, while Paul is saying that trying to do what it prescribes is what leads to curse. The most feasible explanation is that a middle term has been omitted from the argument: people in general, but especially perhaps you Gentiles, are unlikely to be able to keep the law thoroughly, and so you will receive the curse. He says later (5.3) that accepting circumcision is accepting the obligation to keep the whole law; one cannot pick and choose which bits to keep. If you take it on, you take it all on, but Gentiles in particular will find it exceedingly difficult to keep it all.

The second strange thing about his use of the Deuteronomy passage is that in its original context it applies specifically to twelve commandments enumerated immediately before, while Paul extends it to apply to the law as a whole. Such an extension is, however, understandable if we remember that Paul needs a contrast from within the Torah to the Abrahamic blessing, and this passage fits his requirements more nearly than any other.

There is something further that is strange about his argument. Many Jewish teachers and indeed Paul himself in Phil. 3.6 did not appear to find it impossible to carry out all that the law demanded. How far *everything* in v. 10 is to be stressed is now debated.[37] It has been argued that this is not an important part of Paul's case and that there is no emphasis on *doing everything*. The words just happened to be in the piece from Deuteronomy that he wanted to quote for other reasons, namely the juxtaposition of *curse* and *law*, to serve as a foil to the connection between promise and blessing about which he has been talking. Yet the fact that he does quote it suggests that the words do not run altogether counter to what he wants to say. Perhaps therefore we ought not to ignore *doing everything* but neither ought we to give the words undue importance. If one sets out to be 'under law' then one must accept the obligation to obey it (5.3 again). While Paul himself claims to have been not only zealous (1.13–14) but also successful (Phil. 3.6) in keeping it, it would have been very much more difficult for Gentiles to keep it all without moving out of Gentile society. They therefore must be warned not to accept it lightly: this is a little like a divine health warning, but even more like the direction on a bottle of pills that one must take the whole course. We are, it must be admitted, reading more than somewhat between the lines, and the main emphasis in the passage remains the contrast of promise/blessing with law/curse.

In v. 11 we come to the pivot of the argument which is that *life* – by which we must understand life with God, life as the people of God – is gained not by keeping the law but by faith. This is exactly what the story of Abraham was used to show, but now it is shown by a quotation (Hab. 2.4). '*He shall gain life who is justified through faith*', which like Gen. 15.6 is employed by Paul in Romans also. Although the precise way the verse is to be rendered is uncertain, the general effect is clear enough: faith and not law-observance is the necessary and sufficient condition for entering or remaining within the people of God. As with Gen. 15.6, Paul collapses the time of Habakkuk with the time of Christ, and makes the faith of which the former speaks equivalent to Christian faith. Moreover, the verse from the prophet is used to highlight the fact that there are proposed alternative bases for life with God, v. 12. Paul naturally believes that only faith is now the true way and that to opt for law-observance, by itself or as a supplement to faith in Christ, is to desert Christ and the gospel (1.7; 5.4). That law-obedience can be proposed as the way to life with God is supported by the quotation from Lev. 18.5: '*he who does this* (i.e. keeps the commandments) *shall gain life from what he does.*'

The final two verses (vv. 13–14) in this section are among the most debated in the letter. By being crucified, which is taken to be equivalent to having been hanged on a tree, Jesus incurred the curse of the law (Deut. 21.23). It is true that in its original context in Deuteronomy the point of this statement is to warn people not to leave a hanged man hanging overnight because of the curse that would otherwise pollute the land. Paul is interested, however, in the curse as resting on Jesus himself. So when Christ *came under the curse* (v. 13) it was *for our sake*, and by it *he bought us freedom from the curse of the law*. Somehow this was all part of extending *the blessing of Abraham to the Gentiles*. How? What is the exact argument that Paul is mounting? Only a very bold commentator would claim to be sure about the answers to these questions, but what follows is an attempt at an explanation.[38]

The first thing to be said is that in this context *curse* and *blessing* are probably tantamount to being excluded from or included in the people of God.[39] In the immediately preceding verses Paul has been contrasting law and curse with promise and blessing. The curse (exclusion?) is on those who do not observe all that the law requires. However the story of the death and implicitly the resurrection of

Jesus Christ demonstrates the ineffectiveness of the curse or perhaps better the rendering ineffective of the curse. Indeed curse has been turned into blessing for all the faith-children of Abraham, Gentiles and Jews alike. This blessing has come about through the cursed one who defeated the curse (by being raised from the dead), not only for himself but also for those who belong to him. His curse-defeating death (and resurrection) are clearly thus *for our sake*, obtaining for us *freedom from the curse of the law*. In very simple terms, the curse did not work. What was supposed to be curse turned out on the contrary to be blessing. Christians, and in particular Gentile Christians who are not committed to full Torah-observance, have therefore nothing to fear. They have blessing, i.e. they are included.

Finally we come back to where we were in v. 2, to the fact that the Galatians have received *the Spirit through faith* (v. 14). They therefore are God's people. That this is so, and without the need for Torah-observance, has now been argued in three ways: from their own experience, from the story of Abraham, and from showing that while law and curse go together, faith goes with blessing.

It must be conceded that in vv. 13–14 there is no explicit mention of resurrection. Paul leaps straight from quoting Deut. 21.23 to a statement about the purpose of extending the blessing of Abraham. Yet as in vv. 11 and 12 he has been talking about gaining life, and then turns to gaining life despite the curse, it seems inevitable to assume that the resurrection implicitly stands between v. 13 and v. 14.

*   *   *   *

3.6   *that faith was counted to him as righteousness*: Gen. 15.6. It seems reasonably clear in general what Paul is doing with the Genesis passage, but it is difficult to work out in detail how he does it. If we assume that *righteousness* (see above on 2.21) is something like 'the life of the people of God', then Abraham's faith in God's promise could in itself show that he was a true child of God and fit to be the father of many more such children. On the other hand if we stress the behavioural aspect of righteousness, then perhaps Paul is saying that faith was counted to Abraham in lieu of righteousness.[40] If the second interpretation has a slight edge over the first it is because in this passage Paul is contrasting faith with law-obedience, not treating faith as in any sense a form of it. If Paul were saying that

Abraham's faithfulness was counted as righteousness, there would be nothing controversial in his presentation of the patriarch, and nothing new either.

3.8   *scripture ... declared the gospel to Abraham beforehand*: this is not necessarily to say that the entire Christian message was disclosed to Abraham, but that in this one critical matter, acceptance on the basis of faith alone, Abraham was enabled to anticipate the gospel. It is noteworthy that the somewhat parallel passage in Rom. 4 makes explicit use of the fact that Abraham's acceptance by God precedes the institution of circumcision by two chapters in the book of Genesis, but there is nothing of that here. Bruce reasonably enough suggests that the omission may have been made because, like Abraham, the Galatians were being urged to undergo circumcision after being justified, so the less said about the circumcision of Abraham the better.

   '*In you all nations shall find blessing*': this is a conflation of Gen. 12.3 and 18.18. The word for *nations* is, of course, *ethnē*, otherwise translated 'Gentiles'. For Paul, only if justification is by faith can the gospel be truly universal: any supplementary requirement was bound to be discriminatory. To ask for Torah-obedience was to favour Jews and disfavour Gentiles.

3.9   *it is those with faith who share the blessing*: there is no suggestion of alternative tracks to God, a Jewish Torah-track and a Gentile faith-track. Simply, the true children of Abraham and therefore the true people of God are those, whether Jew or Gentile, who have a faith like that of Abraham. The matter is only adumbrated here, but is set out more explicitly in Rom. 4.

3.10   *scripture says* ...: Paul's surprising use of Deut. 27.26 is much discussed. He makes it apply to those who do try to keep the law rather than to those who do not keep it, in contrast to the original context (see for example Betz, pp. 144–6; Bruce, pp. 158–61). As it stands, what Paul says is much more rigorous than was usual in Judaism, suggesting as it does that only one hundred per cent observance of the law will do. In fact Judaism allowed for failure and provided means of atonement. Perhaps Paul is deliberately over-stressing the law's demands in order to drive home to the Galatians that they cannot pick and choose bits of the law to keep, or perhaps (as suggested above) he is trying to make them aware that for them as Gentiles, as not for a Jewish community, full adherence to the law was to all intents and purposes impossible.

3.11   *no one is ever justified before God by means of the law*: it is noteworthy that despite v. 10 Paul does not say that this is because no one can ever observe the law well enough. On the contrary, the reason given is that – as the example of Abraham has shown – law-observance is not and never was the way to justification. This is now underlined by the quotation of Hab. 2.4.

'*He shall gain life who is justified through faith*': Paul's use of this verse does not exactly match either the text of the Hebrew or that of LXX. Moreover, it is not at all certain how we should understand his quotation of it in this context.

(i) REB implies something like 'he that is righteous-through-faith shall live', i.e. it is a statement about justification, about acceptance with God or entry into the people of God.

(ii) On the other hand many other translations, including the Authorized Version, have 'the righteous shall live by faith', in effect thus stating what is the basis of those who are righteous, those who are already accepted by God into his people.

It is possible even on the basis of the present passage, 3.1–14, to argue the issue either way, simply because for Paul both entry into and remaining within God's people are now on the basis of faith. For a very full discussion of the options see Fung, pp. 143f. Perhaps it may be said that (i) is not quite as obviously to be preferred as is often thought.

3.12   '*He who does this* …': it is tempting to conclude from this that Paul is contrasting doing (of any sort) with believing. The law then would represent the 'doing' way to God and Abraham the 'believing' way.[41] While such an interpretation may not be impossible, it does not seem to reflect very well what Paul is doing in this passage: he is contrasting faith with a very specific sort of 'doing', namely obser-vance of the Torah. No doubt he might well have agreed that other forms of 'doing', such as almsgiving or good deeds in general, were equally not the way to justification, but he is not talking about such things here.

3.13   *Christ bought us freedom*: we need not press the metaphor of purchase. There is nothing in this context to suggest any kind of substitution or transaction, let alone with the Devil. Most probably Paul is simply saying that Christ procured our freedom by undergoing the curse and demonstrating its powerlessness.

It is often suspected (e.g. by Bruce, p. 166) that it was his death by crucifixion in particular that constituted a stumbling-block to Jews who were presented with claims of the messiahship of Jesus, cf. I Cor. 1.23. If the messiah was to be God's blessed one then how could this man who had incurred the law's curse be that messiah? If such objections underlie this passage, so also do the church's answers that God's vindication came through the resurrection and that Jesus turned the curse into a blessing.

3.14   *the blessing of Abraham should in Jesus Christ be extended to the Gentiles*: the key to this statement is to be found partly in v. 16 but also partly in the meaning of *in Jesus Christ*. Because Christ is no isolated individual but brings with him those who belong to him and live within his sphere of authority and power (see above on 1.22), what is true of him in this matter is true also of them. They, like him, inherit God's blessing of Abraham. Precisely what this blessing consists in is not clarified; perhaps it does not need to be, for God's looking favourably on people and accepting them as his own is surely enough, together with –

the promised Spirit: for the use of 'promise' see below on 3.16. The gift of the Spirit is clearly part of the inheritance, whereas in Genesis receiving the land of Canaan and populating it was the content of the blessing.

Third argument, from human inheritance
3.15–18

It sometimes happens with preachers that their points are clear enough until they try to provide illustrations. It is then that their hearers may become confused. The same thing can happen with Paul's writing (a famous case in point is Rom. 7.1–3) as it does here. The basic trouble is that he uses the Greek word *diathēkē* which can mean a solemn agreement or covenant, or a 'testamentary disposition', a will. Equally confusingly, 'testament' in English can mean either: we speak of a last will and testament, and we also speak of the New Testament. Which meaning does Paul intend here? The short answer seems to be that he slides from one to the other, a procedure made defensible by the fact that in both its meanings a *diathēkē* can be legally inviolate. A third party cannot alter it. It is likely, however, that the connection is closer than that: God's covenant with Abraham was not so much a legally binding contract between parties, as a divine gift, almost like a 'testamentary disposition' or deed of gift rather than a mutually agreed affair. Indeed it is arguable that in the Bible generally 'covenant' (*diathēkē*) should be thought of in these terms, as divine deed of gift.[42]

If the illustration needs explaining, what it illustrates is comparatively straightforward. Only the testator can alter or add to a will. When God made his promises (his deed of gift, hardly his will!) to Abraham, they were and remain inviolate. They cannot be modified by anything, and that includes the law which came four hundred and thirty years later. At this point there is an unexpected implication that the giving of the law was not unambiguously from God, an implication that will be taken up in vv. 19–20. That this is the implication cannot easily be doubted if we look back to v. 16: the law cannot alter the promise to Abraham because no one can alter or add to a deed of gift or a testamentary disposition. Yet the one who gave the original 'testament' can alter it. Therefore, it seems unavoidable, the law did not come unambiguously from God. Perhaps Paul's illustration has run away from him, but this is what the passage implies.

In v. 16 we are given what is needed to explain v. 14: the promise to Abraham and *his* 'issue' (Gen. 15.5; 22.18) has the word for *issue*, often literally rendered 'seed' and often also rendered 'descendants', in the singular, not the plural. Therefore, Paul argues, one particular person is intended and that particular person is obviously Jesus Christ. So, the promise to Abraham finds its fulfilment in Christ. In the meantime Paul's explanation stops there, but later in the chapter (vv. 27–28) he enlarges the point already latent in v. 14 that Christ is not an isolated figure: he brings his people with him. There is thus a narrowing of the promise to Jesus Christ, and then a widening of it to include Christ's people, Jews and Gentiles together in the church. Yet at this point we are left to fill in this widening ourselves.

So then, the covenant with Abraham rests on faith on the human side, and nothing subsequent can remove that foundation. On the divine side it rests on *promise* and a promise that cannot be rendered *ineffective* (v. 17). We end with another of Paul's either/or statements: *if the inheritance* (v. 18) rests on the law (REB *is by legal right*) then it does not rest on *promise*. But *it was by promise*, therefore it does not rest on the doing of the law. Despite the REB rendering, in this context it is probable that in v. 18 Paul is talking not about *legal right* but about what is required of men and women, viz. faith or doing the law.

*   *   *   *

3.15 *My friends, let me give you an illustration*: literally, 'brothers, I am speaking in human terms'. Cf. I Cor. 9.8; Rom. 3.5; 6.19.

3.16 *the promises*: In Genesis what was promised was above all the land, though naturally also the multiplicity of children, see Gen. 12.7; 13.15, 17; 26.4; 28.13. This has no part in Paul's use of the story, though there may be an echo of it in Rom. 4.13. For Paul the content of the promise is doubtless salvation in general (see 5.21; Rom. 4.13; 8.17; Col. 3.24) but we have already seen that in v. 14 there is a particular emphasis on the gift of the Spirit. *Promise* is not, in fact, an OT term but does emerge in later Jewish writing as a correlate of 'inheritance'.[43]

It does not say 'issues' in the plural: in Genesis it is indeed the singular that occurs, though of course it is a collective singular. In so far as Paul wants the *'issue'* to include Gentile and Jewish Christians as well as Christ himself, in the end he too wants it to be a collective singular. Meanwhile he exploits the absence of the plural to make the single figure of Jesus Christ the single channel of the promise. This may seem a strange argument to us, but it probably did not seem so strange to Paul's readers or even perhaps to his Jewish contemporaries, for there is some evidence (e.g. *Jub.* 16.17f.) of an expectation of one particular individual who would be the true seed (*issue*) of Abraham. See Bruce, pp. 172–173.

3.17 *a law made four hundred and thirty years later*: the figure is, it appears, based on Ex. 12.40 LXX, the length of time Israel 'dwelt in Egypt and in Canaan'. In the Hebrew text, which is the basis of the English versions, four hundred and thirty years is the time spent in

Egypt only. Except that it indicates Paul's dependence on the LXX, this point is unimportant: what matters is that the law is not only subsequent to the promise, but a very great deal subsequent. In at least some Jewish tradition, however, the time gap was unimportant because Abraham kept the law by anticipation (see Betz, p. 158). Paul thus pulls apart and sets in contrast the promise and the law which were in Judaism held together.

It is also worth noticing that, as we shall see again later, while the covenant with God is of prime significance for Paul, the covenant in question is not that on Sinai but that with Abraham. It can hardly be doubted that he is relegating in importance the covenant with Israel on Sinai and with that the importance of the law also.

3.18 *the inheritance*: what is it? In Genesis it is undoubtedly the land, cf. Gen. 15.7, 18–21; 17.8. Paul is not explicit about what it is for Christians, but in the light of the argument of the letter it must be both justification by faith, i.e. membership in God's people, and the gift of the Spirit, cf. 3.6–9, 11, 14. See also the notes on promise above at v. 16.

What place for the law?
3.19–25

After all that has been said against the role of the law, it is almost obligatory for Paul now to add a paragraph about its true role. If this is a digression (Betz, p. 161) then it is one that could hardly be avoided by anyone reared in the Jewish belief that the Torah was the divine guidance for life. Even here, however, Paul's statements are startlingly negative. They are also difficult to understand.

The law was needed in order *to make wrongdoing a legal offence*, v. 19. The argument apparently is that unless there are rules which can be either kept or broken, all wrongdoing is only implicit or potential: it is rather like a disease whose symptoms have not emerged. The law enables the symptoms to appear and then we can perceive the wrongdoing for what it is and know that we are sinners, just as the symptoms enable us to recognize that we are sick. This is a good and ultimately beneficent role for the law. None the less it is a temporary role, for when Christ comes (the *issue*) as the inheritor of *the promise* and the one through whom Gentiles and Jews alike share the inheritance of God's promise to Abraham, then that role is over. That even Christians will need divine guidance and will also need to have their wrongdoing brought into the light of day is true, but is not Paul's present concern. That will be dealt with in chapter 5, but meanwhile it is important to remember that he is talking about not just any collection of rules, but specifically about the Torah.

Its role is not only temporary (*interim*, v. 19); it is also subsidiary. This aspect has already been discussed in vv. 15–18, but is now underlined in an astonishing but obscure fashion. Paul takes up a tradition that the law was communicated to Moses and so to Israel not directly but *through angels*. In that tradition there was doubtless no intention of making it any less directly a divine communication: it was simply a way of talking about that communication without being too anthropomorphic about it. The angels were merely the channel of the communication. For Paul on the other hand, the tradition indicates that the giving of the law was mediated, unlike the promise to Abraham which was unmediated. Indeed he may be saying that there were several mediatorial hands: first the angels together, then a single angelic mediator, and then (presumably) Moses. Alternatively *there was an intermediary* may refer to Moses, in which case the sequence is simply: first angels, then Moses. Either way, this contact between God and Israel is less direct than that of the promise to Abraham.

The statement (v. 20) that *God is one* may mean that this plurality of mediators stands in contrast to the oneness of God. It is possible that behind this statement lies the conviction that God who is one unites Jews and Gentiles into one people, while the law divides them, though this is to supply rather a lot from outside the passage itself. On the other hand it is possible that the line of argument is that *an intermediary* is needed when there are pluralities on both sides and not when there is *one party acting alone*. In the case of the giving of the law, *an intermediary* was needed between the angels on one side and Israel on the other, but in the case of the promise to Abraham there was direct dealing with God himself, the One, and therefore a mediator was not needed.

If the argument is unclear, the upshot is not. The law is not only temporary in contrast with the promise which is permanent, it is also subsequent to the promise without the power to annul or modify it, and moreover it is of less directly divine origin.

Although the apostle has been contrasting promise and law, he now denies that the latter can *contradict the promise*, v. 21. In fact they have different roles. The role of the promise is to give life, life as God's people. This is not the role of the law, for if it were, *then righteousness would indeed have come from keeping the law*, i.e. life as God's people would indeed rest on Torah-obedience. But it does not. Therefore the law has a different role. That role is to demonstrate universal sinfulness in order that everyone should be able to recognize that it must be only by *faith in Jesus Christ* in response to God's promise (here a surrogate for grace) that the *blessing* of being God's people is received, v. 22.

The law's ability to bring sin into the open is a characteristic that Paul discusses elsewhere, see Rom. 5.13; 7.7. However that is not its only role in this passage. Until the coming of *faith* (which here in v. 23 is shorthand for Christ, belief in him, and acceptance with God on that basis) the law was our guardian. In chapter 5 we shall learn that our direction for living as the people of God now comes from the Spirit. Here he is content to say that the old guardianship (*custody*) *of law* is over since the Abrahamic promise has been fulfilled in Christ and his people. Yet while it lasted that old custody was presumably God-given and therefore beneficial; it is persisting in it now that is not only unnecessary but also anachronistic. The REB rendering of v. 24 slightly obscures one of Paul's most interesting metaphors: literally, he says that the law was our guardian up to the coming of Christ, in order that then *we should be justified through faith*. The word for 'guardian' is *paidagōgos*, the slave who took the young child to school and was normally a protector rather than a teacher. This person was essentially a child-minder, who may also have looked after pre-school children. The function was temporary and subordinate; people of responsible age did not need a *paidagōgos*. The metaphor thus expresses rather accurately what Paul was saying about the law: its function was positive enough but subordinate and temporary. That function is now over, and if that seems to leave absolutely no place whatever for the law, we shall see that this is not Paul's last word on the subject.

* * * *

3.19   *It was added to make wrongdoing a legal offence*: a more pedestrian rendering would be 'it was added for the sake of transgressions'. This could be taken in three main ways.

(i) As REB implies and as we have assumed above, the law's function was to expose sin by giving concrete commands, the breaking of which would bring home to people that they were sinners, cf. Rom. 5.13; 7.7.

(ii) The task of the law was to inhibit transgressions, to keep people in check until the time of fulfilment when the Spirit, as the inheritance of the promise (cf. vv. 23–25) could take over that task and do it more effectively.

(iii) On the contrary, the role of the law was actually to produce transgressions, not just in the sense of turning potential sin into concrete sins as in (i), but even to promote sin, thus showing the need for Christ, grace, faith and the Spirit, cf. Rom. 7.5, 8–9, 11.

The last (iii) is theologically difficult in that it apparently makes God the cause of sin at least in the medium term, though not in the long term, for out of it would come true righteousness by faith. Even so, this is a rather extreme interpretation to which we should resort only if others fail.[44] Both (i) and (ii) are feasible interpretations: (i) fits well with what Paul says elsewhere, while (ii) fits well with what follows in vv. 23–25. On the principle that we should look for explanations in the first instance from within the letter in hand before searching more widely, (ii) is perhaps to be preferred and the REB rendering rejected. Nevertheless as we are following the REB version, in the main comment above we have discussed its rendering, not that argued for now.

pending the arrival of the 'issue': does this refer simply to Christ, in line with v. 16, or does it include a reference to those who belong to him, cf. v. 14? It is impossible to be dogmatic, but the word *arrival* does rather put the emphasis on the figure of Christ alone.

It was promulgated through angels: the idea of angelic mediation of the giving of the Law on Mount Sinai is not found in the OT, but it does occur in Acts 7.53; Heb. 2.2. In the LXX of Deut. 33.2 the presence of angels is mentioned. Reference to the idea in other Jewish sources is often uncertain, see Betz, pp. 168–170, and especially Schlier, pp. 156–158. Even if it is occasionally to be found, in Judaism it was not understood to undermine the divine origin of the Law.

It is unlikely that the angels here are bad powers as they were in Gnosticism. Paul's point is simply the indirectness of the process of lawgiving in contrast to the directness of the promise to Abraham.

there was an intermediary: this could be Moses, as clearly in Deut. 5.5; see also Lev. 26.46 LXX. The role of Moses was not taken to imply that the law was any the less from God himself, except apparently by Paul who believes it introduces indirectness.

The other possibility is that the intermediary is simply the angels collectively, so that Paul is saying the same thing twice, or even that it is one particular angel (so Bruce, p. 179) who mediated the work of the generality of angels.

3.21   *righteousness would indeed have come from keeping the law*: i.e. life as the people of God would have consisted in Torah-obedience. The giving of the law does not *contradict the promises*, presumably because their purposes were different: the promise was to give life, but the law was to provide guidance and keep the people in line until the promise found its fulfilment in Christ and his Spirit (see v. 22). This distinction that Paul makes contradicts a basic assumption of Judaism, that the law does give life: see *TDNT*, p. 293, and Lev. 18.5; Deut. 30. 15–20; '*Aboth* 6.7 in the Mishnah; Ecclus. 17.11; also Gal. 3.12 and Rom. 10.5. For Paul, however, life comes from faith (Hab. 2.4, cf. v. 11 above) and promise.

3.22   *scripture has declared the whole world to be prisoners in subjection to sin*: presumably *scripture* is seen as a whole but especially in its role as law. If we ask for a specific passage, then doubtless the answer would be in v. 10 above with its quotation of Deut. 27.26. Literally, the statement runs 'scripture has shut up everything under sin', and there are three main ways in which this can be taken.

(i) As we saw for v. 19, it could be that the law creates sin thus showing the need for grace, or at the very least that it exposes sin by bringing it to light, see Rom. 5.13, 20. This does not seem to be what Paul is talking about here, though it is not impossible.

(ii) Again as we saw for v. 19, it could be that the law inhibits sin, thus keeping people in order until the true solution comes in Jesus Christ, see v. 23 below. This certainly fits the context excellently.[45]

(iii) As REB implies, it may simply be a matter of scripture's declaration that everything, the whole human situation and indeed the whole world, is sinful. The strength of this interpretation is that it emphasizes that it is sin under which everything is 'shut up', while (ii) rather requires that it be the law itself. The only drawback is that the strong language of 'shutting up' is somewhat weakened.

In any case it is noteworthy that in this verse sin is seen not just as doing wrong things, nor just as a wrong disposition of the person, but as a power under which men and women are subjected, cf. Rom. 3.9; 6.12, 14, 16, 20.

faith in Jesus Christ: see the discussion at 2.16 on whether this should read the 'faith of Jesus Christ'. If we take it in the latter way here, then Paul is saying that the believing and/or faithful behaviour of Jesus Christ particularly in undergoing crucifixion is the basis of the fulfilment of the promise. He thus very neatly corresponds to Abraham. In the more traditional view, this expression (*faith in Jesus Christ*) is repetitively underlined by *given to those who believe* at the end of the verse. If it is the *faith of Jesus Christ* this repetition is avoided. As in 2.16, both interpretations are in keeping with what Paul says here or elsewhere, and the disagreement is over just what he is saying at this point.

3.24 *The law was thus put in charge of us*: or 'the law was thus our *paidagōgos*.' We have seen that there is no easy translation of this term, which is presumably why REB has resorted to circumlocution. AV 'schoolmaster' is inaccurate, RSV 'custodian' is better but does rather suggest a caretaker, while NEB's 'a kind of tutor' does tend to imply a primarily teaching role. Not just the appropriate translation of the term, but also the precise scope of the work of the *paidagōgos* is a matter of some dispute[46]. However it seems likely that any teaching role was exceedingly minor, such as hearing the child's homework, and that as a personal slave-attendant his main role was protective. What can be underlined again is that his role was limited and temporary (cf. v. 25) and thus he can represent the law, which protected Israel against corruption and unfaithfulness or something of the sort.

As in v. 23, Paul appears to use *us* inclusively. Strictly speaking only Jews had the Torah *in charge of* them; Gentiles did not. Yet just as in v. 22 the entire universe was in subjection to sin, so here and in v. 23 the law appears to be given a universal role. Whether Paul almost absent-mindedly extends his own experience and the experience of his fellow-Jews to the whole of humanity, or whether he is implying that law in some shape or form played a role among the Gentiles parallel to that of the Torah among Jews, is hard to say. He does appear to generalize his own experience elsewhere, as indeed in 4.1–4.

Fourth argument, the effect of baptism
3.26–29

Baptism is a great leveller, but a leveller up, not a leveller down. After all the preceding arguments for the equality of Jew and Gentile before God, Paul now points to the effect of their common baptism, which renders them *all sons of God*, v. 26. We may wish that he had written in a gender-neutral way of 'children of God', but on the one hand he was a man of his time who puts things in the way natural to him, and on the other hand he is working theologically with Christ as the one issue, the Son, and to maintain the point taken from Genesis he goes on speaking of *sons*. We see from v. 28, however, that he was far in advance of most of his contemporaries in believing that distinctions of gender have at least in principle been abolished.

In v. 26 the word *all* is to be stressed: Jews and Gentiles alike are God's children, and all on the same basis, that of faith. This is on the human side, the way in which they respond to the divine gift. On the divine side, they are God's children *in union with Christ Jesus* (but see the detailed notes for uncertainty about this REB translation). In the light of what has gone before, the point must be that they are no longer under a custodian (*paidagōgos*). Not only are they children of Abraham (3.7) but also children of God, just as Jesus Christ is the Son of God, 1.16; 2.20. It is possible that the change from *we* in v. 24 to *you* in v. 26 signals a change from statements about Jews to statements about Gentiles, so Betz, pp. 185ff., but the change may be fortuitous. It is true that vv. 26–29 have the character of reassurance to the Gentile Christians.

The letter's first explicit reference to baptism comes in v. 27. By being *Baptized into union with him* (or 'baptized into Christ') they entered his possession, see also Rom. 6.3–11. They now belong to him. Presumably, after the descent into the flowing water and their rising out of it, they were given new garments to wear[47] and this is taken to represent their new identity as Christ's people. A similar idea but in different terminology is found in 2.20. It is important to note that especially in this context it is not merely – nor even primarily – a new individual identity, but above all a new corporate identity, as v. 28 makes plain.

So then, within the new sphere of Christ's lordship and power, the old natural distinctions are broken down and the old forms of discrimination are ended. In the everyday world, especially at that time, distinctions between Greek and Jew, male and female, slave and free, were inescapable. Christians were not going to be removed from that everyday world, which is the same as 'the present wicked age' of 1.4. There too the old age had not disappeared, but Christians were fundamentally no longer subject to it, however much they were obliged to live within its constraints superficially. This is now given sharper focus: as Christians they must regard the discrimination that the world takes for granted as for them a thing of the past. Within the present context, obviously the primary point is the absence of discrimination between Jew and Gentile. Paul is not here giving any serious attention to discrimination between slaves and free or between male and female. The fact, therefore, that he does introduce these two other anti-discriminatory matters unrelated to the argument may be evidence that he is quoting something like a primitive formula, perhaps even a baptismal formula, mainly because its first item about Jew and Greek supports his case. Nevertheless, even though he does not develop them here, his statements about distinctions of gender and social status are important, and we have already seen that any tendency to interpret being children of Abraham in purely male terms is effectively undercut by this verse.

The immediate application of this now classic anti-discriminatory verse is (v. 29) that by their baptism and their thus becoming children of God, they equally become *the 'issue' of Abraham and heirs by virtue of the promise*, whether they be Jews or Gentiles. Baptism and what follows from it are as non-discriminatory as is faith. Thus Paul concludes his arguments against requiring Christian Gentiles in effect to become Jews as well.

However, there are implications of v. 28 which are not explored here but which do reverberate elsewhere in Paul's letters. One may think of Rom. 16.7 where the female Junia as well as the male Andronicus is eminent among the apostles, of I Cor. 7.3–4 where conjugal rights are reciprocal and not just of the husband over the wife, and of Philemon where, though Paul sends Onesimus back to his master, thus keeping within the law, he urges Philemon to receive him not as a slave but as a brother in the Lord. Such things are not Paul's main concern in the present passage; all one can say is that the principle enunciated in v. 28 has its effect in other passages. Yet Paul is no revolutionary. He shows no sign of wanting to change the present ordering of society (see Rom. 13.1–7), and what he says here applies to life *in Christ Jesus* only. Nevertheless in the long run it is subversive of that ordering of society.

It must be confessed that the church which has for many centuries rejected any Jew/Gentile distinction within its own community, helped no doubt by the fact that not many Christians were Jewish, yet for far too long declined to accept the same equality for slaves and free in slave-owning societies, and has until very recently also failed to recognize the equality of male and female. This is not something of which the church can be very proud: it has often been better at reflecting the society in which it lived than at challenging that society.

* * * *

3.26 *sons of God*: see the detailed note on 2.20 for the idea of Jesus Christ as Son of God. While doubtless the idea of intimate belonging is present here, Christians are sons (and daughters) of God most particularly in the sense of receiving the family inheritance, see 4.1–7 below. The basic notion that sons (children) should do what their father wants them to do must be taken for granted here too.

in union with Christ Jesus: an alternative rendering of the verse is 'For you are all sons of God through faith in Christ Jesus.' REB in effect breaks the verse up into two separate assertions: you are sons of God by faith, and you are sons of God by union with Christ Jesus. Although these two assertions reflect accurately what Paul is arguing at this point, this is not an altogether natural way to take the verse. It does, however, avoid giving the impression (as the alternative rendering may) that our faith and not God's action makes us his children: in fact our faith merely responds to and appropriates his action. Of course one could well maintain (with Bonnard, pp. 77, 153) that having faith and being in Christ Jesus amount to the same thing.

It is important to note that for Paul human sonship of God is not only parallel to but also derived from Christ's sonship, it is 'in him' that believers exist. This is neatly parallel to their being the 'issue' of Abraham through Christ as the one 'issue'; indeed the two sorts of sonship, of God and of Abraham, are virtually synonymous.[48]

3.28 *male and female*: there is an oddity in the Greek, for while *Jew and Greek, slave and freeman* are all in the masculine, this pair is neuter. The most likely reason for the difference is that Paul is quoting LXX Gen. 1.27 where both nouns occur in the neuter form, 'male and female made he them'. Another indication of quotation is that while the first two pairs are linked by 'nor' (*oude*) the male/female pair is linked by 'and' (*kai*). It would be tempting to suggest that the neuter is employed to show that gender is unimportant, but this would probably be too subtle by half, and in any case the explanation that Paul is quoting LXX is sufficient. None the less some, like Betz, p. 195, do entertain the possibility that the use of the neuter points to the abolition ultimately of biological as well as social distinctions.

you are all one person in Christ Jesus: or 'you are all one in Christ Jesus', REB having supplied *person*, not altogether happily. 'You are all one entity' might be better, for REB's rendering invites the question, 'Which person?' Even if we are to understand a reference to the person of Christ, that is difficult: we can hardly suppose Paul to be saying that the church is the person of Christ (even the body of Chris idea does not mean that). All in all, the traditional 'you are all one in Christ Jesus' seems much to be preferred. For *in Christ Jesus* see the detailed note on 1.22: once again the sense is 'under Christ's authority and within his sphere of power'.

For a discussion of the possibility that in this verse Paul is quoting material that is already traditional, see Betz, pp. 190ff.

3.29   *heirs by virtue of the promise*: if we ask, 'heirs of what?' the answer given earlier (3.14) is 'the Spirit'. This is reinforced below in 4.6, though it is not connected as clearly as we might have expected: v. 6 speaks of the Spirit, and v. 7 of being an heir, yet the explicit link is not made. Perhaps it is that the letter is in general concerned with inheritance in terms of belonging to God's people or family, but is not concerned to be more precise than that.

The fact that this section on baptism concludes with yet another reference to Abraham and his heirs, demonstrates the centrality to Paul's total argument of the story and example of Abraham.

Fourth argument, elaboration and evidence
4.1–7

The idea that Christians, both Jews and Gentiles, are children both of Abraham and of God is now given further treatment in order to explain what it means and how we know that it is true. We begin by going back to the idea of being under custody or guardianship, and by noting (v. 1) that before he comes of age, even an *heir* of vast estates is for practical purposes in the same situation as *a slave*. This continues *until the date set* (v. 2) when his status dramatically changes, even though the higher status has implicitly been his all along. *So it was with us*, says Paul (v. 3). We too have been like slaves *subject to the elemental spirits of the universe*. There are two interlocking problems here: are *we* Jewish or Gentile Christians or both; secondly, what are *the elemental spirits*? For some account of the debate about the latter see the detailed notes; for the moment we shall take it that they are supernatural or even astral powers which at least some Gentiles believed held sway over their lives. If this is right, then the argument probably is that just as the Jews were under tutelage to the law, so the Gentiles were under tutelage to these powers. There is thus a parallelism, so that *we* are all Christians; though we were not all slaves under the same sorts of power, we were none of us free.

However, like a father who sets a time for his son's coming of age, God has his timetable. When he was ready (v. 4) *his Son* Jesus Christ was sent into the world. This need not imply the existence of a second Being beside God in heaven who was then sent into the world from outside, though it may. It may also be simply in parallel to prophetic sending by divine commission, cf. Ezek.2.3; Obad. 1; Mal. 3.1.[49] At all events Christ was the agent of God, and came under normal human conditions or more precisely normal Jewish human conditions: he was *born of a woman* as we all are but also *born under the law* as all Jews are. He came into exactly our situation, not some bogus similitude of it, in order that we should be in effect transferred into his situation, that of sonship (v. 5).[50] As not infrequently in Paul's writings, he came or became like us, in order that we should become like him. In this case the outcome was *freedom for those who were under the law*.

By using as a parallel the situation of human beings under the age of majority, Paul has filled out the ideas of 3.23–25, the *paidagōgos* passage. It is strictly through Christ that we can *attain the status of sons* (v. 5). Once again the argument is worked out in male terms, here especially because it is male inheritance that is taken as the point of comparison, but also once again we need to keep 3.28 in mind.

Now how do we know that all this is true? We know because we have the Spirit (v. 6 and cf. 3.2–5) and this Spirit is not just the Spirit of God but now quite specifically the Spirit of Christ, *the Spirit of his*

Son. For the Spirit as both of God and of Christ see also Rom. 8.9. There is one particular effect of having this Spirit that is crucial to the present argument: he enables us to recognize our sonship so that we cry '*Abba, Father!*' This is how we now naturally address God, see also Rom. 8.15 and Mark 14.36. It is obviously a consciousness of sonship that is not innate (and equally a consciousness of daughtership) but is the gift of the Spirit. We do not need to be argued into this awareness; we have it. It is unwise to make too much of the occurrence of *Abba*. It is true that it is an Aramaic family way of talking that has survived the move into Greek (rather as 'amen' has survived into language after language) and therefore was presumably regarded by the early church as particularly significant. It also cannot be unimportant that in Mark 14.36 it is placed on the lips of Jesus. Yet we cannot say that it was totally unprecedented within Judaism, as has sometimes been claimed,[51] though its importance to the church and to the argument of this letter does not depend upon its being unprecedented.

Finally (v. 7) Paul switches from the plural to the singular, perhaps unconsciously, perhaps to underline the truth of what he is saying for each individual: each of those whom he is addressing is *a son* and *heir* and *no longer a slave*. Once more the male language is dictated by the circumstances that Jesus the Son is male, that the issue of Abraham was male and that heirs were normally male. Once more we must recall 3.28: maleness here is a way of speaking, a way of making the point, but not in itself a substantive point. Once more also we must remember that being a child of God is not just a matter of intimacy or privilege, though that is certainly included, but is also a matter of obedience, of living as the Father wishes. It is still not made exact what it is that is inherited: if in 3.14 the Spirit seemed to be the inheritance, here in 4.6 the Spirit is something like the guarantee of the reality of the inheritance. See again the detailed note on 3.29. Behind all this talk of heirs, we may suspect, lies the idea crucial to this whole letter, namely that of being God's people and sharing his life.

* * * *

4.1 *he is no better off than a slave*: this was not true in every respect, one need hardly say, but it was true in respect of self-determination. In this illustration it seems to be assumed that the father has died, and this is where as an illustration it collapses, for God has certainly not died. All illustrations break down sooner or later, and Paul's are no exception. Details of the parallels are not to be pressed.

4.2 *guardians and trustees*: these are surely parallel to the *paidagōgos* of 3.24f. and so to the law. The two words may be virtually synonymous (see Fung, p. 180), but the first may denote the figure who looks after the child and the second the one who looks after the property, a distinction neatly brought out by REB.

until the date set by the father: this could vary, but 14 was the most usual age, cf. Bruce, p. 192. Paul's phrasing presumably reflects the fact that the father was allowed some discretion.

4.3 *So it was with us*: the almost erratic oscillation of pronouns between 'you' and 'we/us' since 3.23 is hard to explain. It is tempting to distinguish 'you' (Gentile Christians) from 'us' (Jewish Christians), but the parallel between 4.3 and 4.9, with 'we' in the former and 'you' in the latter, seems to make that implausible.

the elemental spirits of the universe: cf. v. 9, and Col. 2.8, 20. This phrase (Greek *ta stoicheia tou kosmou*) is difficult to interpret. The word *stoicheia* can mean 'first principles, elements' of something as it surely does in Heb. 5.12. It can also mean the basic constituents of something, as it appears to do in II Peter 3.10,12. It therefore could here mean the law in parallel with *paidagōgos*, except that 'of the world' (*kosmou*) then becomes very strange, and except that in v. 8 the *stoicheia* seem to be *the gods* that *are not gods at all* which points not to the law but to pagan powers of some sort. Perhaps at the time of Paul's writing the most natural reference is to the elementary substances, earth, air, fire and water, presumably then here standing for the basic forces of the universe. This does not seem to make very good sense.

Therefore the usual view of the meaning of the phrase may very well be right (see Bonnard, Betz, Cousar, Bruce for example). *Stoicheia* came to denote the supernatural forces such as the stars in astrology which control human destiny: this fits what is said in v. 8 and also fits 'of the world'. The only real difficulty with this otherwise rather obvious solution is that it is uncertain whether *stoicheia* had come to have this meaning as early as the time of writing of Galatians. We should have to say that this represents a very early use of the word in this sense. If we may accept it, with some slight misgivings, then Paul is making the bondage of Jews under the law parallel to the bondage of pagans under the astral powers: everyone has been under bondage of some sort and everyone needs liberation from it. Whatever forces ruled their lives, Paul maintains that those forces are now superseded.

4.4 *the appointed time*: or more literally 'the fullness of time'. This corresponds to *the date set by his father* of v. 2, but the fundamental idea is that of salvation history: God works through the processes of history to achieve his purposes, and in that working the coming of Christ is the nodal point. It is not just one more item in a series of divine acts, it is the one divine act which gives meaning and perspective to all the others. There is a note of fulfilment in the phrase which is rather missed in REB's rendering, cf. 3.23, 25; I Cor. 10.11; Mark 1.15 etc. 'The turning-point in the divine-human story' or 'the turning-point in the story of God and his world' would not be too strong as attempts to convey the sense.

4.5 *to buy freedom* . . .: see the detailed note on 3.13, where the same Greek verb is also rendered 'buy freedom for'. The more conventional translation is 'redeem', but in both places REB brings out the sense well.

. . . *for those who were under the law*: on the face of things, Paul is saying that Christ procured freedom only for Jews. What about those, like most Gentiles, who had not been under the law? Are they tacitly included, or does this part of the argument apply only to Jews, or is Paul again ascribing his own experience and personal history to all human beings? The difficulty is compounded if, with most commentators, we assume that 4.1–11 is largely about the Gentile situation before Christ. Is it then possible that in this passage Paul is not only including the law among the *stoicheia* but conversely saying that being under *the elemental spirits of the universe* was tantamount to being *under the law*? Certainly it is virtually impossible to disentangle statements which primarily fit the Gentile situation from those which more naturally fit the Jewish. Perhaps Paul is so emphatically setting out what he sees as the solution, that he is not concerned too rigorously to keep separate the problems which that solution addresses.

in order that we might attain the status of sons: or, 'in order that we might receive the adoption'. 'Adoption' or 'sonship' (Greek *huiothesia*) is found in the NT rather seldom and in LXX not at all: apart from here only Rom. 8.15, 23; 9.4; Eph. 1.5. Adoption was not a Jewish practice, presumably because the sense of family and especially of extended family was too strong for a formal procedure of adopting to be needed. In Roman society, however, it was common and important. Despite the absence of the word from LXX, in the OT the idea that Israel has been chosen (adopted?) by God as his child is clearly present, e.g. Ex. 4.22; Hos. 11.1. It is tempting then to interpret this clause here as saying that in the church Jews and Gentiles together have become the people/children of God, just as Israel did of old. Yet such an idea does not sit easily in this context, where the talk hitherto has rather been of small children reaching their majority (v.1). Perhaps therefore we ought not to stress the idea of adoption, but rather the notion of entering into the fullness of sonship, cf. Bonnard, p.87.

4.6   *To prove that you are sons*: alternatively, 'Because you are sons ...' The Greek *hoti* can be taken either way. Is the Spirit the consequence of being sons/children, or the proof of it? In Rom. 8.19–23 the Spirit is the present guarantee of future sonship, which does not fit exactly with either alternative here. Perhaps (with Bruce, p. 198) we ought to beware of over-systematizing: being God's sons/children and having the Spirit belong together, and the relation between the two can be expressed variously, but we cannot be more precise than that.

into our hearts: it is always useful to remember that in the Bible 'heart' (*kardia*) is not only nor even usually the seat of the emotions, but can stand for almost any aspect of the inner life. It can sometimes denote feelings, but also sometimes the will, and very often the mind, the seat of rationality. It often refers to the person as related to and responding to God, and hence living for him, see *TDNT*, pp. 415f. Appropriately, here *our hearts* are where the Spirit enters, and this should be taken not as restricted to feelings but as including all aspects of our inner existence.

4.7   *by God's own act*: or 'through God' (*dia theou*), an unusual expression for Paul. 'Through Christ' would be more expected. The point may be that everything that has been described in vv. 1–7 is centred on and derives from God himself. No doubt because of its rarity, many MSS have different readings: 'through Christ', 'through Jesus Christ', 'through God in Jesus Christ', to name only the most important. It seems likely (so Metzger, pp. 595f.) that an unusual but not unique (cf. 1.1 and I Cor. 1.9) *dia theou*, 'through God', has been altered by copyists who thought they detected a mistake, and tried to 'correct' it in various ways.

Fourth argument, a critical question
4.8–11

There is only slight advance in content of this section over the previous one. Its purpose is rather to turn the statements of vv. 1–7 into a challenge to those who, as Paul sees things, are inclined to put the clock back. Somewhat confusingly in the light of v. 5 where release is from the law, but in line with v. 3 with its subjection to astral powers, Paul is now certainly addressing former pagans, those who *did not know God*, v. 8. Even when he is most critical of his Jewish contemporaries, he would hardly have said that about them (cf. Rom. 9.4). Moreover their bondage was to pseudo-gods, beings that *are not gods at all*. To *know God* is to be taken in the common biblical sense of being in relationship with him (*TDNT*, pp. 120–22): it is because of this (v. 9) that what is important is not so much that we are in relationship with God but that he is in relationship with us. REB uses the word *acknowledge*, but the Greek verbs are still the same as in v. 8, 'to know'. When God knows a people or an individual, that is to say that he enters into a relationship, a covenant, with them, or even that he elects them, see Gen. 18.19; Ex. 33.12; Deut. 9.24. On the human side, to know God is to acknowledge him (REB is right) and thus to obey him and live for him, see Deut. 4.39; 11.2; Judg. 2.10; Isa. 1.3. Both the human and divine sides of this knowing or acknowledging are important, but God's knowledge of us is prior to and more important than our knowledge of him.

Now that these former pagans are in this rich relationship with God, it would be absurd for them to revert *to those feeble and bankrupt elemental spirits*, cf. v. 3. When Paul asks why they propose *to enter their service all over again*, it is difficult to avoid the conclusion that he regards their placing themselves under the régime of the law as being tantamount to reverting to life under the pagan dominations of their former existence. He is not necessarily identifying the Torah as one of those powers; it is rather that since they have now escaped that bondage and entered Christian freedom, if they accept the law they will enter a slavery which is parallel to but not identical with their former bondage. In effect, 'having escaped from one sort of slavery why do you now want to embrace another?' From the point of view of Paul's gospel, they are contemplating regression. Moreover the two sorts of bondage are not entirely different: both involve observances of *special days and months and seasons and years* (v. 10). In the case of Judaism, the observance was primarily of the Sabbath, but also of feast days and the events of the Jewish calendar. In the case of paganism too there were festivals, but also auspicious and inauspicious days, especially if astrology was a factor in their world view. In Paul's eyes, if these former pagans now embrace observance of the Torah, his efforts to bring them into Christian freedom *may have been wasted*, v. 11.

*   *   *   *

4.8   *you were slaves to gods who are not gods at all*: as this cannot refer to Torah-observance, the case is strengthened for seeing the *stoicheia* of vv. 3, 9 as supernatural forces of some sort. They are not gods, but have been treated as if they were. It may be because of this partly that Paul in good Jewish fashion can on the one hand deny the existence of pagan deities, yet on the other hand perceive them as demonic: compare I Cor. 8.4f. with I Cor. 10.19–22. See also Deut. 32.17, and Betz, p. 215; Bonnard, p. 157.

4.9   *or rather, now that he has acknowledged you*: Paul's self-correction here may simply arise from a wish to make it clear that God's knowledge/election of human beings precedes in time and significance their acknowledgement of him. It is possible, however, that he is guarding against an early form of the Gnostic idea that knowledge (*gnōsis*) of the divine within oneself, as a part of the totality of the divine, is the key to salvation and to escape from the trammels of this vile physical body and this malign universe. Most commentators, however, do not believe that Gnosticism even in an inchoate form was a problem in Galatia.[52]

how can you turn back to those feeble and bankrupt elemental spirits: as in v. 3, the *elemental spirits* are *ta stoicheia*; see the discussion in the detailed note on that verse. In the light of v. 8, these must be the *gods who are not gods*. REB's *feeble and bankrupt* is a decidedly stylish rendering of what is more literally 'weak and poor' and brings out the feeling of the passage admirably. What is particularly noteworthy about this verse is that Paul writes of turning *back* to these powers: unless we are to suppose that he really wants to include the Torah among them, the parallel case interpretation that we have adopted seems the best option. Yet the precise reference of the passage must remain problematic, so that dogmatism is out of place.

4.10   *special days and months* ...: Bruce (p. 204) suggests that the key issue here is calendrical observance. As pagans, the Galatians may well have believed in astral powers that worked on a calendrical basis, as in astrology. In adopting the Jewish Torah they would be adopting a new set of calendrical observances. Although the basis of these was entirely different, to the Galatians it might have seemed that they were back where they started. In other words, the similarities might have struck them more forcibly than the differences. This at least may lie behind Paul's otherwise strange identification of life under the law with life under pagan powers. It is also worth noting that Bruce suspects that the phrase *ta stoicheia tou kosmou* (see on v. 3) used to denote such astral powers, a use otherwise unknown until the second century apart from Col. 2.8, 20, was Paul's own innovation.

Special days must at least include the Sabbath; *months* may refer to the new moons, cf. Num. 28.11–15, though it is hard to see what the Galatians could do about the requirements there set out; *seasons* may be a general term for Jewish festivals. *Years* are a problem, unless with Fung, p. 193 we suppose that the New Year festival is in mind, or rather more adventurously accept the suggestion[53] that the Galatians were observing the sabbatical year of 47/48. One suspects that either the Galatians were being urged to adopt observances the details of which are now beyond our recovery, or (and more plausibly) that the terms are not to be analysed so precisely, but are piled up rhetorically to indicate devotion to calendrical observances.

4.11   *my hard work on you may have been wasted*: the note here is more pessimistic than in 3.4. There is something close to desperation here. Indeed it has been suspected that in the event Galatia was lost to Paul's sort of Christianity.[54]

Fifth argument, personal appeal
4.12–20

If v. 11 betrays Paul's real fear that he may have lost the Galatians to the gospel as he understands it, he now appropriately turns from argument proper and as their founding father straightforwardly implores them, invoking the story of his dealings with them. Un-

fortunately for us he alludes to matters which were common experience between them, but at which we can only guess. What we do
not need to guess is his feeling of deep and agonized anxiety about
them. He appeals to friendship, and urges that as he forwent the
observance of the Torah for their sake, so now they ought to forgo it
for his sake. If we suspect a touch of moral blackmail here, then it
arises from violent feeling and even panic at the thought that he may
be losing them. They have always treated him very well (v. 12), so in
effect he is begging them not to spoil the relationship now. He goes
back (v. 13) to his original evangelization of the area, which came
about (we cannot tell exactly how) because of his *bodily illness*;
perhaps he had an unexpected and unplanned stay in a region which
he had intended merely to pass through. In any case, though they
might have recoiled at his *physical condition* (v. 14), on the contrary
they received him as a divine messenger, or even as *an angel of God*.
His ailment may have been unpleasant in itself, or more probably
they could have interpreted it as a mark of divine disfavour, or even
as a sign of demon-possession. Either of the last two could well have
led them to discount anything he might say, but on the contrary they
welcomed him as God's emissary, just as they *might have welcomed
Christ Jesus himself*. So, despite the very inauspicious circumstances,
the beginning of their relationship was thoroughly happy.

On their side (v. 15) that happiness appears to have evaporated. At
the beginning, they would have given their *eyes* to help him: what
has gone wrong? Certainly (v. 16) he is now being utterly *frank* with
them, but why should that turn him into their *enemy*? Surely, he is
implicitly saying, friendship can survive a little plain speaking? His
undoubtedly strong words in this letter are intended to be signs of
friendship, not signals of its demise.

He contrasts (v. 17) his plain speaking with the blandishments of
his opponents, but the latter are not straightforward, are *without
sincerity*. They are making a great fuss of these Gentile Christians,
but only in order that the latter will turn to them for instruction,
perhaps, in the requirements of a Judaistic Christianity, or even for
the rite of circumcision itself, and so become their debtors in the
faith. The net result of these blandishments, therefore, is the exalta-
tion in importance not of the Galatian Gentile Christians, but of the
Judaizers (v. 17b). It is natural enough that the Galatians should
enjoy being courted (v. 18); who does not? Paul himself enjoys it and
is not alone in that (is it possible that he is being mildly humorous
and self-mocking here?). What is unstated but surely implied is a

warning not to be too impressed by being made *the object of ... attentions*, especially where their sincerity is suspect. In the end the Galatians are not just his friends, but his *own children* (v. 19) in the gospel; he is like a mother who suffered *labour* pains in bringing them to birth as a Christian community. Does he need to go through that *all over again* until they let their lives and their community be completely formed by Christ (and by him alone, is the implication)?

Correspondence is fraught with dangers; written words have an uncompromising character. When engaging in conversation face to face, we can convey nuances and subtleties of tone, so *I wish I could be with you now* (v. 20). As he is not, he is distraught. He simply does not know what to do.

* * * *

4.12 *Put yourselves in my place ... as I put myself in yours*: or, 'Become as I am, because I became as you are.' This could be no more than 'I have become one of you; you then should become (or remain) like me.' In any case the point must still be freedom from the observance of the Torah (cf. I Cor. 9.21) and perhaps especially that observance which respects the identity markers of the Sabbath, circumcision, and dietary restrictions.

You never did me any wrong: this must surely refer to his original visit to them. The likely meaning is, as we have assumed above, that they have treated him well hitherto, so that it is doubly sad that they now propose to desert him and his understanding of the gospel. It is just possible, however, in the light of 2.11–14, that he is saying 'I never came to any harm by eating your food with you, so why should you now find it objectionable?'

4.13 *bodily illness*: this is a ripe field for speculation. It could be related to the 'thorn in the flesh' of II Cor. 12.7–10 which in turn has given rise to much speculation about the nature of Paul's problem. In view of v. 15, some form of eye trouble may seem an obvious candidate, but it is surely more likely that there Paul is simply using a figure of speech for extreme willingness to help. A time-honoured candidate is malaria, and so is epilepsy: the latter is particularly plausible if it was seen as evidence of demon-possession, thus making Paul vulnerable to rejection, cf. v. 14. See Bruce, pp. 208f., for sensible discussion of this whole problem. In fact all speculation is fruitless, if more than a little addictive.

4.14   *you resisted any temptation*: we must beware of over-interpretation at this point, as if some sort of moral temptation were at stake. It is surely no more than 'you did not let my condition be a trial to you'. The Greek is rather convoluted, and REB's translation is as likely as any. In any case the general point is clear enough: they did not let his *physical condition* be a reason for rejecting him.

to show scorn or disgust: the last word is literally 'spit out'. This could reflect a self-protective action, warding against the demons suspected of residing in the ailing Paul, cf. Cousar, p. 100. It could, however, be no more than a figurative way of expressing strong revulsion.

as if I were an angel of God: the Greek *angelos* can mean either an *angel* or any sort of messenger. It is thus possible that we should translate 'as if I were a messenger of God', with the implication 'as indeed I was'. However, if this verse reflects the potential horror at his condition because of the suspicion of demon-possession, then the word *angel* is particularly apt: they received him not as embodying demons but the very opposite. As angels were a particular sort of messengers of God, the notion of his being a divine messenger is present in any case. Cf. Acts 14.11f.

4.15   *you would have torn out your eyes*: see the note above on v. 13. This may have been a proverbial expression for sacrifice of a very high order, cf. Betz, pp. 227f.; Bonnard, p. 93. To deduce that Paul's trouble was ophthalmic may be too literal by half.

4.16   *being frank with you*: literally 'telling you the truth'. While REB's rendering is the more probable, making Paul refer to his thoroughly candid tone throughout the letter, it is also possible that 'telling you the truth' refers to the proclamation of the gospel without adding requirements from the Torah (cf. Bonnard, p. 93).

4.17   *what they really want is to isolate you*: or 'to exclude you'. It seems the Judaizers were telling the Galatians that they were not really or fully within the people of God. In order to be true members they needed to accept circumcision and what followed from it. There is another possibility, that they wanted to isolate the Galatians from Paul (Bruce, p. 211; Bonnard, p. 94); in Paul's eyes this would lead to their being isolated from the true gospel and 'severed from Christ', 5.4. Both these interpretations make good sense, and if the first has a slight edge, one cannot be dogmatic about it.

4.19 *you come to have the form of Christ*: or 'until Christ is formed in you', cf. 2.20; II Cor. 3.18. *You* is plural, and it is therefore possible that Paul is speaking of Christ's being formed in them either corporately or individually or indeed both. In the light of the context which concerns the Galatians as communities, there must be some corporate reference.

Sixth argument, the true descendants of Abraham
4.21–31

Whatever we call this passage, an allegory or a piece of typology or simply an imaginative use of the Genesis story, it is certainly adventurous exegesis of the Old Testament. The aim is straightforward enough: it is to add weight to the conviction that it is those who have faith like Abraham's, whether they be Jews or Gentiles, who alone are his true children. To that extent it serves to recapitulate 3.3–18. The modern Christian reader who is faced with this passage may be tempted to give up in despair, but that would be a pity. For all its strangeness in treating the story of Genesis (16–17; 18.9–15; 21), it does give a sharp insight into how Paul, by apparently turning the story on its head, can claim it for his understanding of the Christian gospel.

It may be helpful to begin by considering what would be a more usual application of the story. Abraham had a son through Hagar, but the legitimate line could not run through that son, Ishmael, for Hagar was a slave. Abraham later had another son, Isaac, by his legitimate wife Sarah; because of Sarah's age and infertility this birth was totally against human expectation, and came about only through the divine promise and the divine action. It was therefore through Sarah and Isaac that Abraham became the father of Israel, and all Israelites traced their descent back to Abraham through Isaac. Ishmael did not come into the picture at all. Further, Abraham was the first to receive circumcision as the mark of the covenant with God, and this circumcision implied the keeping of the Torah (subsequently given on Sinai) as the mark of life within the covenant.

Paul's argument is that this is almost exactly wrong. It is those Christians, Gentiles included, who have the Abraham-type faith

who are the true children of Abraham, because having entered into
freedom they are heirs of the line of the free woman Sarah and her
child Isaac. They belong to the Abraham-covenant of Gen. 15.6, the
covenant of faith, promise and freedom. Rather confusingly, Zion
imagery is also introduced: the Sarah/Isaac/faith/promise/freedom/
Abrahamic covenant/Pauline Christianity line belongs to the
heavenly Jerusalem. Thus what was usually considered the heritage
of Judaism is appropriated by Paul for his kind of Christianity.

Conversely, those who insist on servitude to the Torah belong to
the Hagar and Ishmael line, for that is the line of bondage. The
covenant at Sinai with its giving of the law (see 3.22–25 above) is the
covenant of servitude, subordinate to and later than, as well as less
permanent than, the Abrahamic covenant. Paul's opponents belong
to this lesser covenant and less legitimate line, and to the present
earthly Jerusalem, one which is under foreign occupation and thus in
bondage. Moreover, as there was a tendency to use 'Ishmaelites' as a
blanket term for Gentiles, Paul may even be saying to his opponents:
we are the true Israelites and you are the real Gentiles.

It is hard to think of any part of the Pauline correspondence that
would have been more offensive to his Jewish contemporaries,
whether Christian or not. Not only has he transferred what they
considered their birthright to a group with a high percentage of
Gentiles, he has also treated the holy covenant on Mount Sinai as a
lower and lesser thing than the Abrahamic, instead of seeing it as the
latter's continuation and completion. It is not just that he has
relegated the law in importance, he has even more seriously cast
doubts on the centrality and importance of the covenant as usually
understood. 'What is left?' one may ask. One is tempted to reply,
Nothing. However it will emerge that even in Galatians this is not
quite the end of the matter, see 5.14; 6.2. It is also proper to note that
in Romans the attitude is less negative to the law (Rom. 7.7, 12–16;
8.4; 13.8–10) and also to the covenant (Rom. 9.4; 11.1–32). Nevertheless, the more temperate treatment in Romans cannot obliterate
what is said here.

Towards the end (v. 29) Paul appears to invoke a tradition that as
boys Ishmael and Isaac did not get on well together, and that Ishmael
bullied Isaac. It is therefore not surprising that the descendants of
Ishmael, Paul's opponents perhaps or even the Jewish community as
a whole, are hostile towards and *persecute* the Pauline Christians. Yet
it is these Christians, reliant not on keeping the law but only on faith,
who are the true heirs in freedom, vv. 30–31. This is a similar

conclusion to that reached by a substantially different route in chapter 3. The conclusion is thus not at all complicated; it is the line of argument that is difficult to follow. Some of the details in the passage are also problematic.

* * * *

4.21 *you that are so anxious to be under law, will you not listen to what the law says*: almost certainly the word *nomos* (*law*) is here used in two somewhat different senses. If we take the whole argument of the letter into account, being *under law* must be to observe the Torah as regulation, commandment, and prescription. In that sense the law is classically found in the books of the law, the Pentateuch. Yet the Pentateuch contains much more than commandments and laws. It also contains sacred history, and in the present verse Paul is invoking the law in its sacred history aspect against the law's prescriptive role as it is embraced by his opponents. We recall that for Paul himself the prescriptive role, real enough in its time, is now over, 3.22–25. For a similar use of the two aspects of law, at least on a likely interpretation, see Rom. 3.28, 31.[55]

4.22 *It is written there*: see Gen. 16.15; 21.2–3, 9.

4.23 *born in the ordinary course of nature*: or 'was born according to the flesh (*kata sarka*)'. There may be a double reference, both to a straightforwardly natural birth apart from any supernatural intervention, and also to circumcision which is a matter of the flesh (*sarx*, see 3.3) and which for Paul belongs to the Sinai and so the Hagar line.
    the free woman's through God's promise: see Gen. 15.5; 17.7, 9 etc. In itself it was a natural birth, but conception had not occurred in the ordinary course of nature. In 3.3 the opposition was between 'fleshly' and 'spiritual': here it is between 'fleshly' and 'through promise' (*God's* is not in the Greek text, but has been justifiably added by REB to make the point clear). It is worth noting, however, that in v. 29 the flesh/Spirit opposition does occur.
    It is also important to remember that the promise was for the benefit of all nations, cf. 3.8–9, 14 and Gen. 12.3; 18.18. Behind the tortuous argumentation here lies the conviction that the gospel is for Jews and Gentiles equally, cf. Rom. 4.16–18.

4.24 *This is an allegory*: for discussion of Philo's quite different allegorizing of the story see Bruce, p. 215; Cousar, p. 105. Is this allegory technically speaking, or typology, or what? It is certainly not the sort of allegory that we find in, say, Spenser's *Faerie Queen*. Commentators (e.g. Bruce, p. 217) often suggest it is not allegory but typology because the correspondences are basically historical, and not between things of fundamentally different character. Yet the Greek word need not denote an allegory in the strict sense, and we may be content with noting that the old story is being reinterpreted creatively for a new set of circumstances. The interpretation is ingenious to be sure, so ingenious that we may suspect that Paul was forced into dealing with the story by his opponents, who were using it to argue that just as Abraham, the father of Israel, was circumcised (Gen. 17) so ought Gentile Christians be circumcised.

two covenants: see the exposition of 3.15–18 above. It is remarkable that while indeed the whole argument is only lightly sketched, Hagar and the Sinai covenant receive much more attention than Sarah and the Abrahamic. On the Sarah side we are left to infer a good deal.

4.25   *Sinai is a mountain in Arabia*: the MSS disagree here, many having 'Now Hagar is Mount Sinai in Arabia' or something like it (the variations are quite complex). To say 'Hagar is Mount Sinai' might well have struck scribes as strange, though to be sure something similar is said in v. 24, with the result that they 'corrected' it by omitting 'Hagar'. This is why many texts and commentators disagree with REB and include 'Hagar'.

If, however, we follow REB, to say *Sinai is a mountain in Arabia* may itself seem strange: no Jew would need to be told, and even if some Gentile Galatians did not know the fact, it is unusual to have Paul imparting gratuitous geographical information. Fung (p. 207) may well be right in suggesting that the point is that Sinai is not in the promised land, so that this is another way of relegating it in importance. That Hagar corresponds to the Sinai covenant does not, of course, depend only on this verse, cf. v. 24.

4.26   *the heavenly Jerusalem*: the idea of a heavenly city, parallel to the earthly Jerusalem but without its imperfections, is not uncommon, cf. Heb. 11.10; 12.22; Rev. 3.12; 21.2, 10–27. In the Book of Revelation the city which will in due time be revealed does already exist in heaven: it is thus both future from an earthly point of view and present from a heavenly. The same idea may be detectable in this passage, for *the heavenly Jerusalem* is contrasted with *the Jerusalem of today* (v. 25), though there is no real emphasis on the future nature of the true Jerusalem. Instead the opposition between the two cities is parallel to the opposition of flesh (*sarx*) to Spirit (*Pneuma*), of the merely human to the essentially divine. Thus Paul is saying that though his opponents may justly claim the earthly Jerusalem as their home, he and his churches may equally justly claim the heavenly Jerusalem as their *mother*. For Jewish apocalyptic use of the idea of a heavenly Jerusalem, see Betz, pp. 246f.

4.27 *scripture says*: Isa. 54.1 LXX. This verse became significant in Jewish eschatological expectation (for details see Betz, p. 248). In Isaiah, the barren wife is Jerusalem as she is now, in contrast with her condition in days of prosperity before the Exile. For Paul, the application is rather that the fruitless wife (Sarah) ends up with more children, through promise and the ingathering of the Gentiles into the Christian community, than Hagar, through the normal course of procreation leading to the Jewish community based on the Torah. It seems unlikely that at the time of writing of this letter this was already true, i.e. that Christians already outnumbered non-Christian Jews. More probably Paul is looking into the future with confidence.

4.28 *you . . . like Isaac, are children of God's promise*: as in v. 23, REB has supplied *God's*, quite justifiably as it is implicit. The positive side of the 'allegory' is here made plain. As in 3.6–9, 15–18, it is those who are children of the promise and not of natural descent who are the true people of God, cf. v. 31 and Rom. 4.

4.29 *the natural-born son persecuted the spiritual son*: there are three interlocking issues here.

(i) *Natural-born* and *spiritual* are 'the one born according to the flesh (*kata sarka*)' and 'the one born according to the Spirit (*kata Pneuma*)'. Obviously, as in v. 23 the contrast is between procreation in the ordinary course of nature (Ishmael) and as a consequence of the divine promise (Isaac). There is a close connection between promise and the Spirit, 3.14; 4.1–7. Moreover, throughout this letter there is a considerable emphasis on Christians' having received the Spirit, 3.2–5, 14; 4.6; 5.5, 13–25; 6.1, 8. Therefore although on the surface Paul is simply talking about how the two sons were born, behind that surely is the fundamental dichotomy between merely human life, and life that is centred in God and lived in his power, i.e. the dichotomy between 'flesh' and 'Spirit'. See also above on 3.1–5.

(ii) *Persecuted* and *just as in those days* must surely imply that Ishmael bullied Isaac. In the text of Genesis (21.8–10) when Hagar and Ishmael are sent away it is not said that this was even partly because of ill-treatment of the younger Isaac. Paul's allusion may, therefore, be to later Ishmaelite hostility to Israel, cf. Judg. 8.24; Ps. 83.6. On the other hand there is some later evidence of Rabbinic interpretation in which Ishmael shows rivalry with, teases or even bullies Isaac.[56] Nevertheless we have to accept that we do not know to what exactly Paul is alluding.

(iii) *So it is today* is almost equally obscure. There is no other clear evidence in Galatians that persecution was a problem. It may be, therefore, that the oppression Paul is talking about is the pressure exerted by the Judaizers on the Pauline Christians, trying to make them accept Torah-observance. This we know about; anything else is speculation. *Persecuted* seems an unduly strong word for such pressure, but then in this letter Paul does not hesitate to use strong words (see especially 5.12 below).

4.30 *what does scripture say*: Gen. 21.10–12, not exactly LXX as the word *free* is added by Paul.

Drive out the slave and her son: does this mean that the Galatian churches ought to expel the Judaizers from their communities? Although Paul adopts a more eirenical tone in Rom. 11.13–21 and perhaps 14.1–15.13, the polemical heat of this letter is such that he may indeed be recommending expulsion, cf. Bligh, p. 390. It is also possible, however, that the quotation is aimed not at the discipline of the Galatian congregations, but at the Judgment: the verse is a statement of what will happen then, or even a direction from God to his angels telling them what to do then.[57] If this is correct, then the point is simply to reinforce that the inheritance is for the children of Sarah, not for those of Hagar. Once again we may note that Paul's long-term view can be less exclusivist, Rom. 11.

Exhortation
5.1–6.10

It is inordinately difficult to divide this letter into modes of discourse. According to Betz, we now leave the argumentative part of the epistle and begin the exhortation, what we might today more tamely call the good advice. Yet exhortation has never been far from the surface in any part of the letter, and conversely this present part is scarcely lacking in argument. All the same, there is now a perceptible change of emphasis and the application of the argument is now more dominant and more direct.

Warning against acceptance of Torah
5.1–12

Having been *set free* by *Christ* (v. 1), the Galatians must not now revert, *submit again*, to bondage, even if it is of a different character. Moreover, if they persist in having themselves *circumcised* (v. 2), they will have made Christ of no *benefit* to themselves. Behind this lies the opposition that permeates the letter: either Christ and faith in him, or acceptance of the Torah. The idea that acceptance of the Torah supplements faith in Christ is one that Paul rejects outright. Moreover, the Galatians ought to be aware (v. 3) that circumcision is not a requirement that stands on its own; on the contrary, it implies *obligation to keep the entire law*. The issue thus cannot be just circumcision as circumcision, it is also what circumcision stands for and leads into, namely the totality of life under the Torah. This is why it is an alternative to Christ and faith rather than a supplement: one cannot have both Christ and the Torah as ultimate masters, cf. 2.15–21. If you think that keeping the law is what makes you acceptable to God (*justified*, v. 4), then you have turned your backs on Christ and *have put yourselves outside God's grace*. This is presumably God's grace in Christ, not necessarily outside the grace of God altogether.

Justification by faith leads to life in *the Spirit* (v. 5), as we have seen especially in 3.1–4.6. Because of this (4.7) they await an inheritance, the future nature of which is here underlined: *righteousness*, the fullness of life as the people of God, is something *which we eagerly await*, and await with that confidence in God directed towards the future that the NT calls *hope*. A large part of the letter has been dedicated to demonstrating that the inheritance is by faith and through the Spirit (or through promise). These are what matter: *circumcision* (v. 6) is irrelevant. Belonging to Christ and being within his sphere of lordship and power, being *in union with Christ Jesus*, is to be within God's people. Of course it is not quite sufficient to say that circumcision is irrelevant: it becomes important if people start insisting upon it, as the whole letter shows, but intrinsically it is unimportant. On the human side faith is the only requirement, but genuine faith always has fruit in people's lives, *expressing itself through love*. This may seem an intrusion into the simplicity and starkness of the alternatives Paul is setting out, but in fact it is a vital harbinger of the next section of the letter. If the law is not the guide to life, then what is? The answer will be sketched in 5.13–6.10, but we are here given a foretaste of that answer.

The sequence of thought now becomes rather loose. Paul once again appeals to their progress as Christians (v. 7, cf. 3.2–3; 4.6, 14–15) and rhetorically asks who has *hindered* them *from following the truth*. *Whatever persuasion* (v. 8) made them change their minds and contemplate embracing circumcision and its consequences, that persuasion *did not come from God*. He then appears to quote a proverbial saying about the way in which yeast (*leaven*) rapidly permeates a whole lump of *dough*, even though in itself it is very small (v. 9). He may be saying that accepting circumcision is only one step, but it leads to the permeation of the whole of life by the law, or he may be saying that it takes only a small number of troublemakers to destroy the freedom of the churches. Despite this, and one suspects despite his own fears (3.4; 4.11, 20), he professes *confidence* (v. 10) given him by *the Lord* that they will see sense. Any troublemaker will be dealt with by God.

In v. 11 he very curiously denies that he is *still advocating circumcision*. Why does he need to do this? Perhaps his opponents genuinely believed that he supported their view; perhaps he is looking back to his pre-Christian days when he certainly did advocate it; or perhaps in his earliest Christian phase he did indeed preach a gospel which included the necessity of circumcision and Torah-observance. See further in the detailed notes. At all events he is emphatically not advocating it now; if he were, then he would not be *persecuted*. Presumably it was only a law-free gospel to which people took exception. Whatever he once believed, he now maintains that a gospel which included Torah-requirements would *strip the cross of all offence*. It is not immediately obvious why the cross without Torah-observance would be offensive, but inoffensive with it. When he discussed the crucified Christ in connection with the curse of the law in 3.12–14 there was no suggestion that the scandal of the cross would be lessened were all Christians to accept circumcision. In I Cor. 1–4 there is great stress on the weakness and humiliation represented by the cross, but this aspect is neither increased nor diminished by the fact that many Christians are not circumcised.

The key to this otherwise inexplicable link between the offensiveness of the cross and the rejection of circumcision must surely lie in 2.20 and 6.14: for Paul, Christ and his cross and human faith in him are what together constitute the basis of life, a basis that cannot be replaced nor supplemented by anything else. Unlike 3.12–14, the offence of the cross here is not that it falls foul of a statement in the law, nor even that it falls foul of the usual Jewish messianic expectation, but that it is exclusive. When it is the basis of a person's existence, then everything else is relegated in importance, cf. 6.14 again.

Quite abruptly, in v. 12 we have the most downright rude and even objectionable of all Paul's candid remarks in this letter. In effect he is saying about the Judaizers, 'Why don't they go the whole way and castrate themselves?' This is not an argument, but a cry of exasperation and desperation, and it cannot be an accident that it comes immediately after Paul has once again stressed the exclusive nature of Christ, his cross and faith in him. To add requirements, such as circumcision, is to make the central claim and offer of the gospel not central at all, but an item in a series. That, for Paul, will not do and is to be rejected with all the force he can muster. What he has been arguing more or less objectively throughout the letter now bursts through in the passion that has been threatening to explode at least since 1.6.

* * * *

5.1   *It is for freedom that Christ set us free*: in Greek the sentence is abrupt, lacking any connecting particle. It may be this that has led to the massive textual confusion at this point. REB's text is as likely to be correct as any. The more literal rendering would be 'With freedom Christ has set us free', but while it would be possible with some ingenuity to make sense of this, it is doubtless better to accept that we have an unusual Greek turn of phrase and concur with REB's translation. *Freedom* is the theme of this letter from start to finish, the freedom of the Spirit, the freedom of children who have come of age, the freedom of the true son, Isaac.

refuse to submit again to the yoke of slavery: as in 4.1–11, the Jewish and pagan forms of subjection are seen as parallel. If the ex-pagan Galatian Christians were now to accept circumcision and the law, they would not be returning to the same slavery as before, but they would be returning to slavery none the less. The idea of a *yoke* is not uncommon in religious language for the acceptance of obligations: cf. the yoke of Jesus in Matt. 11.29f, and the yoke of the kingdom, of the law, and also of worldly care in the Mishnah, *Aboth* 3.5.

5.2   *if you get yourselves circumcised Christ will benefit you no more*: for the first time in the letter we are told in so many words that the Gentile Galatians were being urged to accept circumcision and were minded to do so. Why will Christ then be no *benefit* to them? Once again we are seeing Paul's either/or presupposition: it cannot be Christ plus something else for salvation, it must be Christ or some-thing else, though for him the alternative is unreal. There is no other way. To insist on circumcision and the law is to say that Christ is not sufficient, but Christ is sufficient! He then goes further than strict logic and says that Christ would become not only insufficient but also unnecessary. We need to remember that he is not here arguing coolly but expostulating in exasperation, but see also v. 4 and 2.21.

5.3   *every man who accepts circumcision is under obligation to keep the entire law*: this is a perfectly normal Jewish view and simply states what circumcision means, cf. Rom. 2.25. A good and faithful Israelite does not select which items of the law he or she will observe. The question therefore arises, who needed to be told this and told it with emphasis? It looks as if circumcision was being regarded by the

Galatians somewhat as an isolated rite, without taking into account what it entailed in subsequent life. It is even possible that the Judaizers were playing down this entailment.[58] At all events it looks as if the Gentiles did not fully realize what they were taking on.

However we need not take Paul's statement to mean that only perfect observance of the Torah would suffice. Jewish sources which take it for granted that obedience to the entire law is required, none the less routinely accept that in many cases perfect obedience is unlikely: accepting the obligation of the whole law is not the same as doing the whole law perfectly.[59] At the same time it would certainly be much more difficult for Gentiles living in a Gentile environment to observe the whole Torah than it would be for Jews living in a Jewish environment, even one outside Palestine. It is extremely important, therefore, that the Galatians be made aware of what it is they are proposing to accept.

5.4 *When you seek to be justified by way of law, you are cut off from Christ*: it is hard to believe that Paul is talking simply about means of entry into the people of God. After all, he is writing to men and women who are in his view clearly within that people. As in 2.15–21, it is hard to keep separate entry into God's people and living within God's people, which means that it is difficult to reserve *justification* strictly for entry or transfer only. Moreover, Judaism did not believe that keeping the law was the means of entry: that was by God's grace in election, sealed to be sure by circumcision. Keeping the law was how they consequently lived as his people. Here, therefore, the stress may well be less on means of entry than on subsequent living, and the point is that life as the people of God is based on Christ and not on keeping the law.

However, *justified* does usually point to the process of becoming acceptable to God. Perhaps then the Gentile Galatians did erroneously, even from a Jewish standpoint, believe that in order to be truly God's people they must not only have faith in Christ but also accept circumcision and set out to keep the entire law. Perhaps they feared that until they did so they would not be truly and fully acceptable to God and part of his people. Thus, although in Judaism Torah-obedience was not the precondition of divine acceptance, the Gentile Galatians may have thought it was, or so Paul suspected.

outside God's grace: he can hardly be saying that they would be outside God's grace altogether, certainly not if he remembered Deuteronomy with its recurrent emphasis on God's grace to Israel.

Nevertheless, the divine grace is frequently presented by Paul as focussed and uniquely conveyed in Jesus Christ: see 1.3, 6; 2.21; 6.18, not to mention in other letters, e.g. Rom. 5.15; 16.20, 24; II Cor. 8.9; 13.13. If the Galatians accept circumcision and what it entails they are saying that God's grace in Christ is not enough and so, he believes, put themselves outside it. No doubt Paul's opponents saw things differently: for them, as indeed for Abraham, accepting circumcision and Torah-obedience was the natural way to respond to God's grace, not a substitute for it. For them it was both/and, while for Paul it was either/or.

5.5 *by the Spirit and through faith*: on the divine and human sides respectively, these are what make people members of God's family. Nothing further is needed. On the Spirit see 3.2–5, 14; 4.6, 29. On faith see 2.16, 20; 3.2, 5–9, 11–14, 22–26.

we hope to attain that righteousness which we eagerly await: this reminds us that although the letter concentrates on the issue of observing the Torah, behind it is the conviction that a new age is dawning and is already operative for those who belong to Christ, cf. 1.4. Further, the argument in 3.15–29 gains some of its force from the belief that Christ represents fulfilment not only of the ancient promises but also of the processes of history. Here this eschatological view comes to the surface: Christians have received much, but the fullness and fruition are still to come. *Hope* here, as frequently in the Bible, has two characteristics which distinguish it from its ordinary meaning in English. Normally, if I hope something I am somewhat unsure about it, circumstances being what they are. In the Bible hope is secure; it is like faith, but directed towards the future. Secondly, the reason why it is secure is that it is based on God's reliability, in biblical language his faithfulness: he is not fickle but will continue to be towards us what he has already been.[60] *Hope* is therefore full confidence that as we are part of God's people here and now, so at the End (or in heaven, cf. the heavenly Jerusalem of 4.26) we shall be found within that people.

We have taken *righteousness* to mean life as God's people, to be fully realized in the future but already known and enjoyed in the present. It is often taken to mean 'justification', but this is not the usual meaning of the word.[61] A further possibility is that it here refers not to human but to divine righteousness, that saving righteousness that will be demonstrated at the End, hence the reference to *hope* (see Bonnard p. 104). In that case *attain* would be rather inappropriate, for we do not attain but receive or experience God's righteousness, and the verse would be talking rather straightforwardly about the hope for God's salvation.

5.6 *If we are in union with Christ Jesus*: or simply 'in Christ Jesus', which we have taken to mean 'in his sphere of power and authority'. See above the detailed note on 1.22 and also n. 11.

circumcision makes no difference at all: it is easy for modern Gentile Christians to miss the revolutionary nature of this. Hitherto, if there was one thing above all that distinguished the male who was within the people of God, it was circumcision. As for Paul the one essential thing is now faith, and being 'in Christ', circumcision has become almost irrelevant and a matter of indifference, unless people start insisting upon it, in which case it is to be resisted.

faith expressing itself through love: for *faith* see the detailed note on 2.16. Although it is essentially response to God's action and his offer in Christ rather than anything active, it cannot remain passive but must issue in the sort of life that befits that response. It can do this, as Fung points out (pp. 230–32) because the life of faith is life in the Spirit of Christ who gives power, see 2.20; 3.1–6; 5.22. This new sort of life is based on *love*, see also 5.22; Rom. 5.5; I Cor. 13. Love is the fulfilment of the Torah, 5.14; Rom. 13.8–10. It is noteworthy that in these passages it is love of one another that is stressed; perhaps love for God goes without saying, or perhaps (cf. I John 4.20) love for one another is the way in which love for God is to be expressed. Apparently it is taken for granted that the Galatians will know what such love means in practice, though some indication is given in 5.19–21. It is likely that all the ethical material from here to 6.10 is dominated by the idea of love (*agapē*), see Betz, p. 263. One thing is certain: in the Bible love is not to be confused with either passivity or sentimentality. It is active and practical, though how it will operate in any given situation must in the end be worked out by people in that situation, remembering that they themselves are recipients of God's love, cf. 2.20. There is already in this verse a hint that such love is not merely something to be striven after, it is *faith expressing itself*, and we have noted that this is because it is the fruit or harvest of the Spirit (5.22).

The triad faith-hope-love, so familiar from I Cor. 13.13, is also to be detected here, in this and the previous verse. It may well have been a regular Pauline habit to juxtapose the three terms, see I Thess. 1.3; 5.8; Rom. 5.1–5.

5.9   *'A little leaven ... leavens all the dough'*: as the same saying occurs also in I Cor. 5.6, many have wondered if it was a contemporary proverb, though one that is otherwise unknown. The secret and pervasive effect of yeast (*leaven*) is normally in the Bible a metaphor for bad influences, though in Matt. 13.33/Luke 13.20–21 there is an instance where it is a metaphor for the Kingdom.

5.10   *The Lord gives me confidence*: is he really confident? We noted a distinct lack of confidence in 4.20. Perhaps the point is that, although the situation in itself can only make him afraid, the Lord and the Lord alone can give him confidence. *The Lord* is presumably Christ; a reference to God would make sense here, but as a rule of thumb we can say that *the Lord* is Christ when Paul is composing his own words, but is God (Yahweh) when he is quoting the OT. He is not quoting here.

whoever it is who is unsettling your minds: does the unmistakable note of vagueness arise from genuine ignorance of the exact identity of the troublemakers, or from a reluctance to name names for some reason? It is unlikely that he is hinting at eminent persons, from Jerusalem for instance: in chapter 2 when he disapproves of Peter's action he does not hesitate to name him.

must bear God's judgment: presumably at the End, though see the *anathema* (ban, curse?) in 1.8–9.

5.11   *if I am still advocating circumcision*: in the exposition above we briefly noted that there are three possible reasons for this denial.

(i) It could be a reference back to his conventional Jewish past, cf. 1.14; Phil.3.6 (and Bruce, p. 236).

(ii) It could reflect a genuine belief of the opponents that they were in line with Paul's real views and normal practice.[62]

(iii) It could refer to an earlier phase of Paul's Christian mission when he proclaimed a Jewish Christian gospel, and then did expect Gentile converts to be circumcised and commit themselves to the Torah, cf. perhaps II Cor. 11.24 and even Gal. 1.18–24 which could fit with a closer relation to the Synagogue than is usually supposed.[63]

(iv) There is a further possibility, not mentioned hitherto, that it reflects an accusation that Paul could preach circumcision when it suited him (cf. I Cor. 9.20 perhaps), and so was denying the Galatians the full gospel. This could conceivably find an echo in the circumcision of Timothy, Acts 16.3.

None of these options is impossible. The most obvious answer is (i), but we must admit that we simply do not know against what precisely he is defending himself. What we do know is that he denies that he now accepts the necessity of circumcision, but it is to be noted that he never objects to the circumcision of the male infants of Jewish Christians.

why am I still being persecuted: for his tribulations see II Cor. 1.5–6; 11.23–26; Phil.3.10; Col. 1.24. As in II Cor. 11, the present context implies that he was in danger from his own people, surely because of his attitude to circumcision and to the Torah in general.

Warning against corruption; the guidance of the Spirit
5.13–24

Up to this point Paul has been concentrating on the issue of the law and of circumcision, and has been insisting that what gives the Galatians entry into God's people and constitutes their life as that people, is not Torah-observance but faith in Jesus Christ. God's acceptance of them is sealed by the gift of the Spirit. Now the apostle turns more concretely to the sort of life that must characterize their belonging to God and to Jesus Christ, and in this passage he works out the opposition between 'flesh' (*sarx*: what REB calls *your unspiritual nature*) and the Spirit. It cannot be too strongly emphasized that this is not an opposition between two existing parts or two aspects of normal human beings, but rather is a contrast between two centres, bases or orientations of the human person. At its most fundamental it is an opposition between life under and for God, and life under and for something that is not God (for both 'flesh' and 'Spirit' see above under 3.1–5). The nature of the opposition between these two kinds of existence is clearer here than anywhere else in Paul's writings, for the list of the 'works of the flesh' (REB *the behaviour that belongs to the unspiritual nature* v. 19) is obviously not a list of physical sins. They are certainly included (vv. 19, 21) but so are sins of the misuse of the supernatural (v. 20) and above all sins of human relationship (vv. 20–21). Wrongness towards God, wrong use of the physical body, but especially wrongness in our dealings with one another are the things that betray our living 'according to the flesh' or our indulging in the behaviour that belongs to the unspiritual nature. *The harvest of the Spirit* (v. 22), on the other hand, is not about fostering the higher faculties we are supposed to have, but is about letting God through his Spirit work in us. To repeat, this passage is not about lower and higher aspects of the human being, but is about alternative orientations, the God-centred as against the merely human.

It is sometimes suggested that in Galatia Paul was faced not only by Judaizers who wanted to impose the Torah on Gentile converts, but also by libertines or antinomians who believed they had freedom to do whatever they pleased without restraint. On this view, Paul in the present passage turns to fight this second set of opponents.[64] We know that sometimes such an inference was drawn from Paul's gospel, whether or not in good faith (Rom. 3.8; 6.1). However there is no sufficient reason to suppose that Paul had to fight on a second front in Galatia, and it is entirely possible that he is simply guarding his exits, so to speak: he is no fool, and knows well enough that his sort of gospel could be vulnerable to misuse by people who do not want to take holy living seriously. Moreover, people need some sort of guidance for life, and if the law is no longer to be that definitive guidance, then the Galatian Gentiles must be given something to take its place. If not the law, then what? This passage provides at least the outline of the 'then what'.[65]

The answer comes not just in terms of orientation, of living in the Spirit instead of in the 'flesh', for the love command stands like a rubric over the whole passage, vv. 6, 14. The beginning is appropriately enough the matter of *freedom* (v. 13). Much of the argument until now has been to show that his readers were free from the powers of this world, from elemental 'spirits of the universe', and from the law and its curse, and implicitly also from sin.[66] However central to Paul's gospel this freedom is, it could carry with it the danger that the element of rescue from sin is undervalued, the danger of corruption into self-indulgence or *licence for your unspiritual nature*. Being free from the regime of the law does not mean being free from the demands of morality; it merely means that the law is no longer the ultimate standard of what is to be done and what is not to be done. That ultimate standard is now the *love* command (v. 14) in which *the whole law is summed up*. This obviously cannot mean that everything in the law is included in or even derived from the love command: duties towards God are not included, for instance, and plainly Paul would not wish to include things like the command to circumcise male infants. No doubt many of the more universally moral of the law's commands are implied in the command to love, the laws against killing and adultery for instance, but there is a vagueness about the expression *summed up* which may be deliberate. Perhaps the point is on the one hand that if we love one another we shall in fact do a great deal of what the law commands, whether we are aware of it or not, but on the other hand that not necessarily every particular commandment need be observed (see further in the detailed notes).

Needless to say the love commandment is itself taken from the law, Lev. 19.18. This demonstrates that the Galatians' freedom from the law as a regime does not carry with it freedom from everything that is found in the law.

The strife within the Galatian churches (v. 15) is evidence that this love of neighbour needs to start within the Christian communities themselves. We have not heard much about this strife, but it comes to the surface here and may underlie the considerable stress on community relationships in the list of vices, vv. 20–21, and to some extent also in the list of virtues, vv. 22–23. However, as such lists tend to be conventional, it is unsafe to make too much of the precise items to be found or not found in any given list.

In v. 16 we discover what undergirds Christian morality, now that the Torah is not the definitive guide and sanction. Christians are those who live by God's Spirit (cf. 3.2–5, 14; 4.6). They therefore cannot any longer live by or for anything less than God, which is what *your unspiritual nature* amounts to. Indeed, what is centred in and based on God is inevitably at odds with life centred in and based on anything else (v. 17): in the end, it all amounts to the inability to serve two masters. Neutrality is tacitly taken to be impossible, so we need to choose which master we will serve. If (v. 18) we choose *the Spirit*, then the Spirit is the one under whom and by whom we live, and there can be no power-sharing: we cannot at the same time also have the *law* as our ultimate authority.

Yet if the Spirit is the ultimate guide and authority, we still need some idea of what this means in practice. In providing this, Paul does not introduce a modified set of commandments and certainly not an altogether new set, but instead provides two pictures. The first picture (vv. 19–21) shows what life is like when lived without God at the centre, and when we look at this picture it comes down pretty much to extreme self-centredness. The second picture (vv. 22–24) shows what life is like when centred on God through his Spirit. To draw his pictures of these alternative ways of life Paul uses a quite conventional method: he gives lists of vices and virtues. As a method of ethical teaching this is not much favoured in our culture, but in Paul's world it was familiar. We have already noted that we cannot deduce too much from precisely which virtues and vices are mentioned and which are not, so that, for example, it is doubtless not particularly significant that in the vice list there is no mention of dishonesty. Vice lists were intended to represent all vices, and virtue lists to include all virtues, whether actually mentioned or not. Nevertheless such lists could have emphases, and these ones have very interesting emphases.[67]

The behaviour pattern of the *unspiritual nature* (or perhaps better, 'the ungodly life') is obvious, v. 19. The list begins with sins that are essentially physical: fornication, indecency and debauchery. This is much what we should expect, especially if we remember the older translation of v. 19, 'Now the works of the flesh are plain' (RSV). The list continues, however, with idolatry and sorcery (v. 20) which are religious sins, sins of wrong worship and of the exploitation of the supernatural. We then (vv. 20–21) have eight items which are all in one way or another social sins, such a predominance possibly reflecting problems in the congregations, cf. v. 15. In the usual English sense things like *envy*, *fits of rage* and *selfish ambition* are not 'works' or sins of the flesh. Even *unspiritual nature* (REB) could unfortunately suggest that something basically physical is at stake, but while the physical side of sinning is included, it is clearly not dominant in this list. At the end (v. 21) we do return to sins of indulgence, *drinking bouts, orgies, and the like*. So much then for the portrayal of life that is centred on our own appetites and ambitions, our own self-importance even. This sort of life has no place in *the kingdom of God*: even if observance of the law cannot earn a place in the people of God, it is still the case that evil deeds can result in exclusion from the life of heaven (the probable meaning of *the kingdom* here).

The REB renderings of vv. 19 and 22 slightly obscure an interesting contrast. In v. 19 we have 'the works of the flesh' and in v. 22 'the fruit of the Spirit'. If the first is what we do, the second is what God does in us. Further, 'works' are plural but 'fruit' (or *harvest*) is singular, pointing perhaps to the disintegration and divisiveness produced by the one, and the harmony and unity produced by the other. One must say 'perhaps', as the variation in number could be by chance and not significant. The first fruit of the Spirit is notably *love*, cf. vv. 6, 13–14; I Cor. 12.30–13.13, and after *joy* and *peace* which may be primarily Godward qualities, the other items on the list are to some extent focussed on community relationships, or more simply on how we get on with one another. They are the converse of the central block of the works of the flesh, v. 20. When Paul goes on in v. 23b to say *against such things there is no law*, one is tempted to reply, How could there be? The clause is undeniably difficult: unless we suppose that *against* is not the appropriate translation of the Greek preposition here (see the detailed notes), the meaning may be something like 'life under the regime of the Spirit may entail ignoring circumcision and the food laws, but it also leads to love, joy and the rest, and they most certainly do not infringe any law'.[68]

We end with a theme that is prominent elsewhere (Rom. 6.1–14; Col. 2.12–3.4) and was introduced in this letter in 2.19–20, the theme of being crucified with Christ. The old self, responsible for *the behaviour that belongs to the unspiritual nature* (v. 19), has died as it has renounced its old allegiances and escaped from its old dominations and desires (v. 24). It is true that here Paul does not say that our crucifixion is 'with Christ', but see 2.20. The old way of life, with its self-centred *passions and desires*, listed in vv. 19–21, is dead.

* * * *

5.13 *your unspiritual nature*: or the 'flesh' (*sarx*). In 3.3 this same term was used for circumcision, there translated *the material*, and in both places it is set in opposition to the Spirit. Presumably therefore there is an intrinsic link between opting for circumcision, and living for one's own appetites and ambitions, since both are forms of *sarx*. Yet in most respects they are obviously different. One arises, in Paul's eyes, from over-valuing the law in God's new day, and the other from having standards that are emphatically too low. The most obvious suggestion to account for their apparent equivalence is probably also the best: anything that is based other than on the Spirit of God, whether in itself good or bad, is *sarx*. It is less than the best that God has to offer.

5.14 *the whole law is summed up in a single commandment*: or 'the whole law is fulfilled in one saying'. There are several issues here.

(i) Is *the whole law* the same as in v. 3, where Paul says that those who are circumcised ought to keep the whole law, not picking and choosing within it? We argued above that he can hardly mean every bit of the law in that sense here (the Greek words for 'entire'/'whole' in the two passages are different, but it would be precarious to infer too much from that). We can only with great difficulty suppose that the apostle is saying 'every single thing in the law is implied by or included in the love commandment'. We know for certain that he regards some things as expendable, e.g. 6.15 and circumcision.

(ii) The use of the word 'fulfilled' (Greek *peplērōtai*, REB *summed up*) may be significant. Usually in the Bible one keeps, observes or does the law. One does not 'fulfil' it, though there is an exception in Matt. 5.17. This makes one wonder if it is carefully chosen to do two things.[69] First, it conveys the idea that like the law, love is a matter of doing, and more exactly of doing what God wants. Secondly, it implies that we have reached some kind of completion, that the aim of the law has been realized and a consummation attained. Yet it does not follow that every single item in the law still has to be observed: this is why Barclay's suggestion of deliberate ambiguity is attractive. It allows for the sense that the aim of the law in living for God is achieved by love, but does not commit us to retaining the law as the definitive guide to the divine will.

(iii) This is the letter's first positive mention of the law. We may wonder why Paul need bring it in at all at this point; perhaps as his opponents had put it so firmly on the agenda, he felt obliged to relate Christian ethics to it in some way. Perhaps he has not wanted to jettison the law as thoroughly as the letter has until now implied, and in effect now says 'Look, the command to love conveys what the law is aiming at, namely the doing of God's will. Love one another, and though you do not need the law, at least it was pointing in the right direction.'

(iv) The practice of taking a few commandments, or only one commandment, to give the essence of the law in a nutshell is well-known both in the NT and in Jewish sources, e.g. Mark 12.28–31 and parallels; Rom. 13.8–10; in the Babylonian Talmud Sabbath 31a (R. Hillel on Lev. 19.18) and Makkoth 24a, the last containing a classic attempt to summarize and simplify the Torah. Yet it must be stressed that in Jewish sources the aim is to find the one commandment or the few commandments which can imply all the rest, not enable the rest to be dispensed with. Whatever Paul is doing when he uses the word 'fulfil', he can hardly be saying that the love command leads into all the other commands.

5.15 *if you go on fighting one another*: this points to some sort of factiousness within the Galatian churches, but what sort? It is tempting to say that the issue must be the necessity or otherwise of accepting circumcision and Torah-obedience. While that is not impossible, the difficulty is that the letter hitherto has given the impression that the Galatians were all too undivided on the issue. The reference to being *conceited* (v. 26) may point to the same sort of hyper-charismatic superiority that Paul tried to counter in Corinth, but there is no further evidence of such an attitude within this letter. In short, we may guess at the cause of the strife but we do not know what it was.

5.16   *be guided by the Spirit and you will not gratify the desires of your unspiritual nature*: or, 'walk by the Spirit and you will not carry out the desire of the flesh'. For 'flesh' (*sarx*) see above on v. 13 and 3.3. The translation *your unspiritual nature* is satisfactory so long as we remember that 'spiritual' ought to have a capital letter: 'Spiritual', i.e. based on and living under God's Spirit. We are not dealing with the physical in opposition to the immaterial, e.g. the soul. The unspiritual nature is basically life-without-God, life not centred in God. The cure for such life is not the law, but life in the Spirit, as the passage proceeds to spell out.

We also need to remember 1.4 and the announcement of rescue from the present evil age. This is the age of *sarx*, 'flesh', while the new realm into which we may be delivered is the age of the Spirit. There is thus a strongly eschatological dimension to the 'flesh'/ 'Spirit' contrast throughout the present passage: not just higher and lower ways of life, but also the life of God's future in contrast with the life of the discredited past. This helps us to gain more understanding of how *sarx* can be used both for life under the law (3.3) and for all kinds of immorality and self-indulgence, whether physical or otherwise (vv. 19–21).

5.17   *They are in conflict*: the whole of this verse presupposes a battle between two forces. Obviously the Spirit of God is a force or power, but it is important to observe that so is *your unspiritual nature* (v. 16), i.e. *sarx* or 'flesh'. We are not talking simply about two different orientations, one towards God and one away from him. We are also talking about two powers under which we may live, very closely parallel to the powers of God/righteousness and sin in Rom. 6.12–22.

so that you cannot do what you want: In our main comment on the passage as a whole, we have taken this to mean that we cannot with unrestricted freedom decide our courses of behaviour. On the contrary we are always under one power or the other; what we do have now is the freedom to choose which power we shall serve. Real freedom, in other words, is being able to choose the better power.

However both the translation and the interpretation of this clause are contentious.

(i) REB treats it as a result clause (*so that* ...) but it could be a purpose clause ('in order that you be unable to do what you want'). In this latter case, presumably the conflict arises because the Spirit inhibits our following the 'lusts of our unredeemed nature' (v. 16). Although the Greek (*hina mē* followed by the subjunctive) is more naturally taken as a purpose clause, surely the verse as a whole implies that it is the conflict as such, and not specifically the Spirit, that inhibits our doing what we wish. A result clause has therefore a good deal to be said for it.

(ii) It is natural for us to think of Rom. 7, where also there is an inner conflict. Yet in that passage the Spirit is not mentioned until 8.2, and appears more as the one who resolves the conflict, not one of the participants. At least part of the time in Rom. 7, the conflict is between sin and the commandment, with the 'flesh' relatively passive and 'I' basically on the side of the commandment but ineffective and powerless. Here in Galatians 'I' is the battleground between the two opposing forces. The similarities between the two accounts of inner conflict are thus not as close as at first appears.

(iii) Behind the interpretation that we have inclined to adopt above lies the view that our moral choices are defined by the battle between 'flesh' and 'Spirit', or between our *unspiritual nature* and *the Spirit* of God.[70] On the one hand we do not have an infinite or even a very large number of options from which to choose, let alone absolute freedom. On the other hand we are faced with alternatives: this, or that; what is for God, or what is against him.

5.18 *you are not subject to law*: we may again, as in v. 14, wonder why Paul needs to mention the law at all. Although it may seem like an intrusion, it is not. We are still with the basic issue, if the law is not the definitive guide to living any longer, then what is? Paul's answer is, the Spirit. In that sense the law and the Spirit are alternatives. It is a question of which authority the Galatians are to accept as paramount. Moreover, we shall see that the list of things that belong *to the unspiritual nature* (vv. 19–21) is by and large not a list of infringements of the Torah. Indirectly, many of them can be regarded as implications of lack of love, which is an infringement of the Torah. More directly they are probably simply to be seen as manifestations of evil. The law does not deal with them, but the Spirit does.

5.19 *the behaviour that belongs to the unspiritual nature*: more traditionally, 'the works of the flesh are manifest'. For parallels to this list and for the ancient use of catalogues of virtues and vices see Betz, pp. 281–3, and Bruce, p. 247.

fornication: Greek *porneia*, a term which could be specific for intercourse with prostitutes, but could also denote sexual immorality in quite general terms.

indecency: Greek *akatharsia*, which can include fornication, but can also be used of reprehensible behaviour outside sexual contexts. It was often used for impurity in the technical sense, but here is most likely to be a moral term.

debauchery: Greek *aselgeia*, which has a field of reference difficult to distinguish from the previous two terms. The piling up of terms is more for rhetorical effect than because subtle distinctions can be made between them. If we must make distinctions, then perhaps this word has an extra connotation of blatancy.

5.20 *idolatry*: hardly a word we should expect to find in a list of pagan vices, but one that to the Jewish mind was absolutely basic, and a typical charge to be made against the pagan world. See also Rom. 1.18ff.

sorcery: Greek *pharmakeia*, essentially manipulation of the supernatural for one's own advantage or others' disadvantage. Its etymological connection with 'pharmacy' correctly indicates that drugs were often involved, though needless to say the word could be used in a quite neutral or even good sense.

quarrels: hostile feelings and actions, especially actions. Once again we may note that the terms are heaped up for effect, without there necessarily being sharp distinctions between them: see below.

a contentious temper: Greek *eris*, strife or discord.

envy: Greek *zēlos*, which can be either good or bad, 'zeal' or 'jealousy'. Here it is obviously the latter, one of the most unattractive of all vices, and one which is all too easily given a more respectable name, like 'a sense of fairness' or 'justifiable resentment'. It is a mistake to think too narrowly of sexual jealousy, important though that may be. With REB, *envy* is therefore the most appropriate rendering.

87

fits of rage: Greek *thumoi*, a plural not uncommonly used for outbursts of anger.

selfish ambitions: this renders a Greek word (*eritheiai*) that is so rare that we cannot be sure of its meaning. 'Disputes' is a possibility, but the more likely meaning is 'a mercenary attitude, selfishness', despite its being in the plural.

party intrigues: the Greek is *haireseis* from which our English word 'heresies' comes. Cliques and factionalism, little different from the immediately preceding *dissensions*, are what it denotes.

5.21   *jealousies*: one wonders why this is plural. Perhaps it refers to outbreaks of jealousy in the community. The fact that this is virtually a repetition of *envy* (v. 20) underlines the rhetorical nature of a list like this. Nevertheless this word (*phthonoi*) is not an exact synonym for *zēlos, envy*: the latter can be either good or bad, but this word cannot have a good sense.

At this point some MSS add *phonoi*, 'murders', which obviously is close in sound to *phthonoi*, and in another Pauline list (Rom. 1.29) immediately follows it. There are important textual witnesses both for and against 'murders', but the most likely explanation is that originally the word was lacking and was added by scribes who remembered Rom. 1.29. REB is justified in omitting it.

drinking bouts, orgies: Greek, *methai* and *kōmoi*, the basic idea being revelry that has got out of hand. *Kōmoi* were originally festal occasions and not reprehensible at all, but in the NT the word always occurs in juxtaposition to drunkenness (see Rom. 13.13; I Peter 4.3). We should think not of sexual orgies, which are covered in v. 19, *debauchery* etc., but rather of systematic over-indulgence in food and drink.

and the like: a general expression to cover all other bad things that have not been specifically mentioned. We must again note that the absence of some particular vice is not significant. Those that are mentioned are representative of all. Nevertheless it is striking that the list as a whole has a strong orientation towards what destroys good and healthy community.

as I warned you before: when? Presumably when he was with them, perhaps during their baptismal preparation. *Warned* translates *proeipon* which could also mean 'predict', a meaning that would fit here almost equally well.

no one who behaves like that will ever inherit the kingdom of God: the kingdom of God/heaven is a common topic in the synoptic gospels, but is comparatively rare in the Pauline literature. Although it may be too much to say that in Paul it always refers to God's future kingdom (probably in heaven), where we read of 'inheriting' it, it must surely do so. See I Cor. 6.9, 10 where the warning is closely similar to that here, and I Cor. 15.50; Eph. 5.5. In the Community Rule of Qumran (1QS 4.11–14) there is a similar warning at the end of a list of vices. Such things as are in Paul's list matter because they matter eternally.

5.22 *love*: Greek *agapē*, unlike its cognate verb, is relatively rare outside biblical literature. Its Christian use is essentially for love that is disinterested, not grasping or possessive but generous and giving. It is used for God's love towards us (e.g. Rom. 5.5, 8) but most frequently for Christians' love of others (e.g. 5.6, 13, on which see the comments above; I Cor. 13; II Cor. 8.7, 8; Phil. 2.1–2, etc.).[71]

joy: Greek *chara*. This is not a matter of being obstinately cheerful on all occasions; after all there are plenty of occasions when we do better to mourn. If we look at the contexts in which Paul writes of joy or rejoicing, they are to do with confidence in God for the future (Rom. 5.2), or with being reconciled to God (Rom. 5.11), or with gifts of God or his Spirit (Rom. 14.17; 15.13; even Phil. 2.29). This basic joy can survive difficulties and sufferings (II Cor. 7.4; 8.2; Col. 1.11; I Thess. 1.6). One might suggest that in the Bible there is a time for joy and a time for sorrow, and in its proper time and place neither inhibits the other. Dare one go further and suggest that the true manifestations of joy are not the fixed grin nor the insensitive refusal to be decently sorrowful, but an underlying courage and a sense of humour?[72]

peace: Greek *eirēnē*, cf. Hebrew *shālôm*. While it is true that *peace* denotes absence of conflict, with one another but above all with God, that is not the whole story. In the Bible it regularly denotes total well-being, both in relation to God and in relation to other people. It thus often includes connotations of health and of prosperity. So when Paul invokes peace on his churches, as he regularly does, he is invoking blessings that are comprehensive: see the openings of all his letters, and often elsewhere, e.g. 6.16; Rom. 2.10; 5.1; 14.17; 15.13, 33; II Cor. 13.11; Phil. 4.9; I Thess. 5.23. The reference is above all to a healthy relationship to God in the first place, and between Christians in the second.[73]

patience: the Greek *makrothumia* could almost be rendered 'long in the temper'. In the Bible this is a quality of God (e.g. Ps. 103.8;

89

Rom. 9.22) as well as of humans (I Cor. 13.4; I Thess. 5.14) and is to be set in contrast with the *fits of rage* of v. 20. This is not to deny that there can be a place for anger, and certainly there is a place for 'the wrath of God' (e.g. Rom. 1.18). In this very letter Paul has a sustained anger from start to finish. Even so anger is to be kept in restraint, and the fuse ought to be long rather than short. Perhaps we can add that it is important that anger should not arise from self-regarding concerns.

kindness: once again a quality of God as well as of humans, cf. Ps. 34.8; 136.1; Rom. 2.4; I Cor. 13.4.

goodness: a word with a very wide range of meaning, but probably here having connotations of generosity (so Bruce, pp. 253f.).

fidelity: the Greek is *pistis*, which in Paul usually means faith, and in particular that faith which is the human response to the divine gracious offer. That meaning is highly unlikely here, so that REB is wise to prefer the perfectly possible 'faithfulness' or *fidelity*. Even 'reliability' would do. God too is faithful (Rom. 3.3) but the context is about human qualities.

5.23 *gentleness*: the Greek *praütēs* is traditionally rendered 'meekness', but this is unfortunate for it tends to suggest being rather feeble, or in modern slang 'wimpish'. The idea is the absence, indeed the opposite, of arrogance, and of strength which is not used to bully. See Matt. 5.5, where the meek/gentle will inherit the earth. The idea of gentle strength is well brought out in the lines of Shakespeare, *Measure for Measure* Act 2 Scene II:

> O! it is excellent
> To have a giant's strength, but it is tyrannous
> To use it like a giant.

The term occurs in other lists, cf. Eph. 4.2; Col. 3.12; Titus 3.2; James 1.21; see also I Peter 3.4, 15. In practice it must be similar to patience, v. 22.

self-control: the Greek *enkrateia* is sometimes rendered 'temperance'. This also is related to gentleness in that one restrains one's strength. Although it often has sexual connotations (cf. I Cor. 7.9), the reference here is probably quite general, with sexual self-discipline no doubt included.

Just as the 'works of the flesh' were dominated by the mishandling of social relationships, perhaps particularly within the Christian community, so the 'fruit of the Spirit' has a strongly community-oriented character. If the first list is a portrayal of the wrong way to live, and to live together, the second list depicts the godly way to live and to live together in the community.

Against such things there is no law: we have already discussed this briefly, and noted that the statement rather invites the question, 'Whoever thought there would be?' This has led to the suggestion that the word *kata* here translated *Against* ought somewhat unusually to be rendered 'in relation to'. If we adopt this suggestion, then the sentence as a whole says that this important list consists of things which the law cannot take into account. There is not and cannot be any law which says 'Thou shalt be meek/gentle', for instance. In the nature of things not all behaviour can be governed by law, whether we think of the Torah or of law in general, and it is exactly such crucial matters as these which fall outside its purview. If law, or the law, does not cover such things as are in this list, then Christian behaviour cannot find its ultimate guide there. The Spirit is thus needed not only as empowerment, but also as definitive guide. This is an attractive suggestion that may well be correct.

There are, however, two difficulties. First, in terms of normal usage it is very much more likely that *kata* means *against* and not 'in relation to'. Secondly, it is not altogether true that the things listed in the *harvest of the Spirit* are outside the purview of the Torah, whatever may be true of other legal systems. In their way they are all outworkings of love, and love is commanded in the Torah (cf. 5.14, quoting Lev. 19.18). Therefore, despite its attractiveness and despite some distinguished support (see Bruce, p. 255), this interpretation must remain uncertain.

In the main comment on the passage we assumed that *against* was the appropriate translation, and suggested that the point is that the Spirit leads not only to infringing things like the command to circumcise, but also to things like love and joy, and there is certainly no command against them.[74] Put positively, there is a lot in common between the morality found in the Torah and the morality led by the Spirit; in practice the conflict between them is limited.

Neither interpretation is altogether satisfactory, yet neither can be regarded as impossible. On balance, taking *kata* to mean 'in relation to', so that the fruits, of the Spirit are things which tend to lie outside the sphere of law, seems to be not only more straight forward but also to give the easier sense.

5.24 *Those who belong to Christ Jesus have crucified the old nature*: we have noticed that crucifixion with Christ may be implied here, but is not made explicit, contrast 2.19–20; Rom. 6.6; Col. 2.20. Another striking difference in this passage is that here Christians are the agents of their own crucifixion, not the objects (cf. Barclay, p. 117).

Verse 25 serves as a link between the foregoing passage and what comes next. It could equally well be included with either.

Further exhortation, a series of maxims
5.25–6.10

After the tight structure and clear progression of the passage immediately preceding, this one gives a somewhat miscellaneous impression. The maxims all fall under the heading, however, of living by the Spirit (v. 25). If God through his Spirit is the basis of Christian existence, then this will have a constant effect on ordinary living. It is closely parallel to faith expressing itself through love, 5.6. It is often, moreover, pointed out that the indicative 'you are in the Spirit' or *the Spirit is the source of our life*, issues in the imperative 'live by the Spirit', or *let the Spirit also direct its course*. Conversely, the command to live by the Spirit can be obeyed only by those who are already in the Spirit. Indicative and imperative are reciprocally related to one another.

If the list of the effects of the Spirit in 5.22–23 has given a general and inevitably rather vague picture of living by the Spirit, what now follows is much more concrete and much closer to detailed cases. In the maxims from 5.26 onwards, there is room for debate about how far they are simply echoes of Hellenistic moral advice, how far they have been forged by Paul himself, and how far they are Pauline adaptations of standard contemporary wisdom.[75] We may think, however, that it is the context of this advice in the new life that is important, not whether there is anything altogether distinctive about any particular item of advice.

A crucial setting for the new life given by the Spirit is the Christian community itself, and that is the sphere for much that now follows. Christians must not think of themselves as being in any way in competition with one another (5.26): there is no place for pride, jealousy or rivalry. On the contrary there must be mutual support, especially when anyone is caught out in wrong behaviour (6.1), recognizing that the person who now gives such support may need to receive support on another occasion. Temptation affects everybody, which means that support must be given *gently*, not as if from the morally superior to the inferior, which is a form of patronage. In thus supporting one another (carrying *one another's burdens*, 6.2), we are in fact doing what Christ wants. The *law of Christ* is an unparalleled expression whose precise meaning is uncertain, but provisionally we may take it to mean 'the law as focussed on love, in line with Christ's teaching and example'.[76] See the detailed notes. If this is correct, one of the prime examples of living by the love command and at the same time bringing to fruition that sort of life under God at which the law was aiming is the supportive way that Christians treat one another.

A degree of realism is needed in our estimate of ourselves, v. 3: too high an estimate is not only a sign of pride, it is also self-*deluding*. If we *examine* our *conduct*, we should do so not by *comparing* ourselves *with anyone else*, but in terms of what we ourselves ought to be and do (v. 4). In the last resort we are accountable for ourselves (v. 5), presumably to God, but see the detailed notes. We cannot use somebody else as an excuse, e.g. 'at least I am better than so and so'.

At v. 6 there is an abrupt changes of theme: those who are *under instruction in the faith* ought to be prepared to give material support to the teachers who are supporting them in Christian matters. Then another abrupt change in v. 7 brings the observation that actions have consequences, and God is not to be hoodwinked (*fooled*). To go back to 5.19–25, if we live for the *unspiritual nature* ('the flesh', *sarx* yet once more) which is perishable by its very nature, then our life itself is perishable (v. 8). On the other hand if we live for God through his *Spirit* who is by nature eternal, then we shall find *eternal life* ourselves. Therefore (v. 9) we ought to be diligent in *doing good*, i.e. living in the way that is appropriate to those who are in the Spirit, in order to *reap our harvest* of imperishable life. Finally, in v. 10 it is underlined that the community itself is the primary setting for doing good. It is not that those outside the Christian community are excluded from consideration (*let us work for the good of all*), but they are not where consideration begins.

* * * *

5.25 *If the Spirit is the source of our life, let the Spirit also direct...*: or 'If we live by the Spirit, let us also follow (in the way of) the Spirit'. REB brings out the nuances well. See also vv. 16, 18.

5.26 *We must not be conceited*: was there a sense of charismatic or even Gnostic superiority in some Galatian quarters? There is very little sign of such an attitude in this letter, in contrast to I Corinthians. It could be a quite general piece of advice, one which religious people in most communities need to hear, without there having been any particular bearing on the Galatian churches. On the other hand v. 15 does imply some cause of strife in Galatia, which may be reflected here.

6.1 *If anyone is caught doing something wrong*: the Greek is ambiguous. It could be a matter of being caught out, or caught up, in doing wrong. REB opts in effect for being caught out. Either way, whether one is caught out, caught up, or perhaps even both, the process of putting things right must be done not arrogantly but with sensitivity. Presumably here we are dealing not with flagrant and outrageous wrongdoing, but with relatively minor matters, for Paul's attitude to serious wrongs is quite different, at least it is in I Cor. 5 and the case of the man's living with his father's wife. How one knows which faults are in what category the NT does not tell us, but later the church developed a distinction between mortal and venial sins. We may be given a clue here, however, in that *something wrong* (Greek *paraptōma*) is probably an isolated action and not a settled course of behaviour (see Bonnard, p. 117). It is in any case important that we here see that Christians despite their being in the Spirit can do wrong things. It is not expected that they will be entirely free from failures, notwithstanding the sharp antitheses of 5.13–24.

gently: literally 'in a spirit of meekness/gentleness'. See above on 5.23.

6.2 *Carry one another's burdens*: we shall discuss the possible conflict of this with v. 5 when we come to the latter verse. As a maxim it is not unprecedented (see Betz, p. 299). The *burdens* (Greek *barē*) are the burdens of everyday life: it is possible that financial problems are meant, but in the context (cf. v. 1) it is more likely that we are still in the realm of moral and behavioural difficulties (see Bonnard, p. 118). Paul calls for mutual moral support, though that need not exclude support of other kinds, even financial.

in this way you will fulfil the law of Christ: we may first note that some MSS have not the future indicative, which lies behind the REB rendering, but the aorist imperative, which would give the translation 'in this way fulfil the law of Christ'. See Metzger, p. 598. On the whole the future indicative is to be preferred, with REB.

What is *the law of Christ*, and what is meant by *fulfil* here? There are several points to be considered.

(i) We saw at 5.14 that the verb 'fulfil', there rendered *summed up*,[77] is unusual in that the law is normally 'done' or 'observed' or 'practised', but not 'fulfilled'. There may therefore well be some connotation of things' having been brought to completion, some idea of consummation.

(ii) In view of the similarity of this verse to 5.14, it is hard not to conclude that the law of Christ and the law of love overlap, if indeed they are not synonymous. In that case this is one of the relatively few places where Paul betrays awareness of the gospel tradition, and in particular of Christ's summary of the law in terms of the love commandment, see for example Mark 12.29–31.

(iii) Nevertheless it has been suggested that the law of Christ is simply the whole teaching of Jesus, at least on its ethical side (so Bruce, p. 261). While such a reference would be hard to disprove, it must be less likely than (ii), if only because there has been no mention of any such tradition in the letter, while only a little earlier the love command has certainly been described as fulfilled (5.14).

(iv) It is possible (Betz, p. 300) that Paul borrowed the expression from his opponents, who may have used it to argue that followers of Jesus the Messiah ought to be diligent in observing the law. Paul then uses the same expression quite differently, interpreting it in the light of the love command in 5.14 and the whole passage about the Spirit from 5.16 onwards. Love and life in the Spirit thus achieve that life under God at which the law aimed, except that they do it more successfully (cf. 3.23–25). This can be no more than a possibility, but it does help to explain why Paul used such an unusual expression, one which does not sit altogether easily with his normal usage.

The phrase does thus remain puzzling. The key to its elucidation probably lies in a combination of (i) and (ii): the law of Christ is the law as brought to fulfilment in love, and as exemplified and taught by Christ.

6.4 *he can measure his achievement*: or 'his boast is in himself alone and not (in comparison with) someone else'. REB brings out the sense well. Is this here and now, or at the Judgment? In the light of v. 5 it is possible that we should think of the latter.

6.5 *everyone has his own burden to bear*: or, to bring out the future tense in the translation, 'everyone will bear his own burden'. There is apparently a contradiction between this verse and v. 2: do we bear one another's burdens or do we each bear our own? Perhaps the future tense here is the key: in v. 2 we may have the sharing of the burdens of everyday life, but here that standing alone before God which occurs at the Judgment. There are different words for *burden* in the two verses, but it would be precarious to build much on that. The most feasible solution is that in v. 2 Paul is talking about mutual support in the community (cf. v. 1), but in v. 5 about every person's situation before God, whether in the present or in the future (see v. 4, and Bonnard, p. 175).

6.6 *he should give his teacher a share*: the exact sense of this whole verse is not easy to identify. The meaning could be as in REB, i.e. that people who are receiving Christian instruction should support their teachers in material things, cf. Luke 10.7; I Tim. 5.18 and especially I Cor. 9.14. In practice, Paul did not always take advantage of this principle himself, cf. I Cor. 9.15–18; I Thess. 2.9. However, it is just possible that *the good things he has* are not material resources but spiritual blessings; it is even possible that the verse is saying that the taught should share in all the good things the teacher offers, i.e. make the maximum use of the teacher. Of all these, the interpretation implied by the REB translation is the most likely.

What were they taught? Doubtless the Christian tradition, as for example in I Cor. 15.1ff., but also perhaps ethical teaching of the kind just given in 5.16–25.

6.7 *God is not to be fooled*: more traditionally, 'God is not mocked'. This may be in answer to any who thought that since the gospel is free of conditions, a libertine style of life is permissible for Christians. Paul is then saying that we cannot fool God: actions do have consequences, even perhaps eternally and at the Judgment. Genuine faith issues in loving actions (5.6): the sowing of faith leads to the reaping of love, and love is a matter of deeds. However not everything in the letter has to be a rebuttal of wrong ideas, and we cannot confidently deduce from this verse that there were libertines in Galatia. It may simply have been something that Paul wanted to say for its own sake.

everyone reaps what he sows: a common maxim, cf. Bruce, pp. 264f. Is this in conflict with justification by faith, not works? If our understanding of Galatians is correct, Paul does not downgrade good deeds as such. He rather denies that works *of the law* are required for entry into and remaining within the people of God as now redefined through Christ. Good and loving deeds remain essential for those who claim to have faith in Christ, cf. 5.6, 14. In any case, the idea that Judgment is in the light of how Christians have lived is found elsewhere in the letters: II Cor. 5.10 for instance is quite explicit about this. We might say that the proof of the pudding is in the eating, and the proof of the faith is in the living.

6.8 *eternal life*: in contrast to John's Gospel (e.g. 17.3), *eternal life* in Paul's letters is strongly future, and denotes life with God in heaven. See Rom. 2.7; 6.22–23, and probably Rom. 5.21. The expression is relatively more common in the Pastoral Epistles than in the un-disputed letters: I Tim. 1.16; 6.12; Titus 1.2; 3.7. In the present verse there may be a reflection of believers' sharing in the resurrection of Christ (see Rom. 8.11, and Bruce, p. 265), but as the whole passage vv. 7–9 seems to have an eschatological orientation, the time of such sharing is probably at the Judgment (Bonnard, p. 126).

6.9 *doing good*: see above on v. 7, and reaping what we sow. In the context, *doing good* gives content to sowing *in the field of the Spirit* (v. 8) and shows that love has to be worked out in concrete behaviour (see also v. 10).
    we shall in due time reap: note the future tense. The time in question is doubtless God's time, i.e. at the consummation.

6.10 *as opportunity offers*: this could mean 'whenever we are given the opportunity', as REB implies. Perhaps less probably, it could also mean 'while the present time (before the End) continues' (so Cousar, p. 146; Bonnard, p. 127). In this latter case, the implication is that they should not view the imminence of the End as an excuse for doing nothing, but as an additional spur to loving actions.
    let us work for the good of all, especially members of the household of the faith: we can probably take this at its face value as a quite general admonition. It is possible but unlikely that it refers to the collection for the poor in Jerusalem, cf. Rom. 15.37; I Cor. 16.1–4; II Cor. 8.3–4; 9.1–15, and see above on 2.10. One would have expected such a reference here to be more explicit.

Postscript
6.11–18

The body of the letter is now complete. The remainder is written in Paul's *own hand* (v. 11), which implies that the bulk of the letter is not. In Romans (16.22) we are told that Tertius did the actual writing, but here no scribe is named. Indeed no one other than Paul himself is named either at the opening or at the closing of the letter. Needless to say there has been much speculation about why Paul wrote in *big letters* (v. 11), but the short answer has to be that we do not know. What is interesting for the study of the process of writing and dissemination of the letters is that this verse implies only one copy, which a messenger then carried round the churches of Galatia and read to each in turn. This seems much more likely than that there were multiple copies and that Paul laboriously wrote out the same quite lengthy postscript in each of them.

The passage adds little to what has already been said. Paul does now, however, clearly impugn the motives of those who are urging the Galatians to accept *circumcision*: they want to remain *in good standing*, presumably with the Jewish community, and so avoid the hostility faced by those who rely solely on Christ crucified (v. 12). That he suspects this is a device, and not a serious intention to ask for full observance of the Torah may be indicated by the word *outwardly*: contrast 5.3, where he stresses that circumcision entails accepting the full obligation of the Torah. Somewhat confusingly he then says (v. 13) that in practice these people themselves *are not thoroughgoing observers of the law* but want the Galatian Gentiles *to be circumcised* in order to enhance their own self-esteem (*boast*). How this could be so is not clear, unless we recall 4.17 and the charge that the protagonists of circumcision were bolstering themselves by the number of people they were bringing round to their view. It must be admitted that the passage sounds as if Paul's anger is boiling over and that vituperation is replacing argument, not for the first time (cf. 5.12). This sort of charge could be brought against any evangelist or the advocate of many a cause. None the less it is of a piece with the expressions of fierce anxiety and resentment that are a sporadic feature of this letter, cf. 1.6–9; 3.1–4; 4.11, 15–20; 5.10, 12.

If his opponents are bolstered up by the number of human trophies they can win, Paul himself (v. 14) is bolstered up by one thing and one thing only: *the cross of our Lord Jesus Christ*. By sharing in crucifixion, Paul has died *to the world*, to the present age, cf. 1.4; 2.19–20. What matters now (v. 15) is not whether or not one is circumcised, but whether one is part of the *new creation* brought about by Christ. It may seem odd that at the end of a letter full of arguments against imposing *circumcision* on Gentile converts, he should say that it does not matter either way. The answer must be that it does not matter whether one is a circumcised Jew or an uncircumcised Gentile, but it does matter if people start insisting that the uncircumcised must become circumcised, in effect that Gentiles must become Jews. That insistence must be fought. In short, circumcision is unimportant until someone makes it important, utterly wrongly in Paul's view. Yet it must be emphasized that he never criticizes Jews for being Jews, nor argues that they ought not to be circumcised.

His acceptance of circumcision for Jews may be underlined when in v. 16 he invokes *peace and mercy* on all who assent to the *principle* that circumcision is a matter of indifference, and specifically includes *the Israel of God*. Although it could denote the church as the new Israeli this could well be historical Israel, the Jews whether Christian or not. Paul is not antagonistic to historical Israel (see also Rom. 9–11) but does strenuously object when any attempt is made to impose its distinctive obligations upon his Gentile converts.

Finally, just before the standard blessing of v. 18, he almost pathetically begs for no more trouble, on the grounds that in the course of his ministry for Jesus Christ he has already suffered enough (v. 17). That there are no greetings to individuals, or from his own associates, is a notable feature of this letter. This highly unusual omission underlines, if any underlining is by now needed, that this is a thoroughly polemical letter, written in passionate heat. His bitter tone may be regretted, but the depth of his concern cannot be denied. So far as the Galatians are concerned, he fears for the gospel. At least at the very end he calls them his *friends*.

*   *   *   *

6.11   *how big the letters are*: the most obvious reason is simply that Paul's handwriting was larger than average, certainly larger than that of the scribe who wrote most of the letter. Almost inevitably, however, it has been suggested that his eyesight was poor (see above on 4.1), so that his script had to be large for him to see what he was writing. Another explanation could be that he wrote large for emphasis.

6.12   *those who want to be outwardly in good standing*: literally 'those who want to make a good showing in the flesh (*sarx*)'. REB's rendering is not the only possible one. *Sarx* ('flesh') could refer to circumcision rather than to outwardness, as in 3.3 (REB *the material*). The point would then be that by persuading others to accept circumcision they increase their standing, perhaps in their own eyes or perhaps in the Jewish community. Then the desire for good standing is the same as the desire to avoid persecution. REB's translation, on the other hand, rather suggests two separate desires, one for outward standing and one for the avoidance of persecution.

to escape persecution for the cross of Christ: although it is not said from whom persecution was feared, it is almost certainly from their fellow Jews. This persecution could arise from political motives: those who fraternized too freely with the uncircumcised could be suspected of not being truly patriotic in the mood of the times. It could also arise from religious motives: Jewish Christians could be suspected of not being strict about food laws in their social relations with the uncircumcised. In either case *the cross of Christ* is a kind of shorthand for reliance on faith in Christ crucified and on him alone.

It is not likely that at this date persecution by the Romans was the source of fear. Of course, as followers of a crucified rebel they might be regarded by the Romans as dangerous revolutionaries, and it is possible that they could escape this suspicion if they could plead that they were merely practising Judaism of a particular sort. All the evidence in this letter, however, is that Paul's opponents were concerned not with their relations with the pagan government, but with their relations with their fellow Jews. See also above on 2.12.

6.13   *those who do accept circumcision*: the Greek participle (*hoi peritemnomenoi*) is ambiguous. It could refer to the Gentile Christians who are accepting circumcision, or to those Judaizing Christians who are trying to impose circumcision upon them (cf. v. 12).[78] Despite REB, the latter is more likely, for Paul's next remark has much more significance if the people who are not good *observers of the law* are the very people who are urging circumcision, than if they are those who have succumbed to the urgings. If would be hardly surprising if people who have only just been circumcised were not (yet?) thorough in their observance, and hardly worth commenting upon.

are not thoroughgoing observers of the law: if the comment on the previous section of the verse is correct, Paul is saying that even the Judaizers who are trying to impose circumcision are not themselves devoted observers of the whole Torah. It is a point of some importance if they are content to impose the entrance rite without worrying too much about what follows, or ought to follow.

Perhaps circumcision was being treated as a sop to Jewish militants; perhaps there were some who genuinely thought that nothing else mattered anything like as much as circumcision; it is even conceivable that circumcision was being treated as a mysterious rite, Gnostic fashion, which was being adopted for its own sake without regard to its proper context in Torah-obedience. The last is not likely, despite some arguments in its favour[79], because there is no hard evidence that Gnosticism was a problem in the Galatian churches. Probably the most likely explanation is none of the above, but simply that Paul was being rude about his opponents, that he is indeed talking about the Judaizers rather than their victims, and that he is accusing them of themselves not being very devout keepers of the very Torah that they are recommending to the Gentile Christians. It would hardly be the first piece of straightforward rudeness in this letter.

to boast of your submission to that outward rite: or 'to boast in your flesh (*sarx*)'. REB neatly brings out the force of the Greek, cf. v. 12 and 4.17.

6.14   *God forbid that I should boast of anything but the cross of our Lord . . .*: as quite often in Paul's writings, the word *boast* here strikes us a little strangely. How does one boast of *the cross*? By saying in effect 'My God is better than your god'? Hardly. Although 'boast' is a quite normal lexical equivalent to the Greek verb *kauchesthai*, it is apt to jar a little, as it does here. This is why in the extended comment above the words 'bolster up' have been used instead, a trifle colloquially no doubt, but intended to convey more than a hint of 'reliance upon'. Cf. I Cor. 1.31; II Cor. 10.17.

the world: Greek *kosmos*, cf. 4.3. *World* has almost the status of a power, a power in opposition to God, perhaps the same as *the present wicked age* of 1.4, and even *the elemental spirits of the universe of* 4.3, 8–10. It is not the universe astronomically speaking, nor exactly the totality of human beings, but an organized power both natural and supernatural which is set in contrast with God. In order to avoid impugning the divine creation, we might speak of it as the fallen world, not the world as God made it to be.

is crucified to me and I to the world: there is no need to look for some subtle difference between the two crucifixions. This is a rhetorical way of emphasizing the total and radical break between two forms of existence, the old age and the new (1.4), *your unspiritual nature* and *the Spirit* (5.16–25), between living without Christ and living by faith in him (2.19–20). This is certainly not to say that Christians cannot delight in the natural and human worlds: indeed they should enjoy them more than anyone else. It is to say that Christians' lives are under God and for God alone, not under or for anything else whatsoever. See also Rom. 6 and Col. 2.20–3.11.

6.15 *the only thing that counts is new creation*: cf. II Cor. 5.17. The idea of a new creation is closely akin to the idea of a new humanity, conveyed by Christ as the last Adam, cf. Rom. 5.12–21; I Cor. 15.21–22, 45–49. As Paul sees it, Christianity is not so much a new religion as a new way of being human, the true and definitive way at that. On such a vision of what the Christian message entails, it is not surprising that circumcision becomes irrelevant, cf. 3.26–28. Whether one is a Jew or a Gentile (or slave or free, or male or female) is a distinction that pales into insignificance beside the crucial distinction of whether one lives in the new age, the *new creation* or the old. For the idea of new creation see Isa. 65.17; 66.22; Rom. 8.19–23.[80]

6.16 *peace and mercy*: as Paul began the letter with a curse or ban, so he now ends it with a blessing, cf. 1.8–9.

the Israel of God: the precise reference is disputed, and there are two main possibilities.

(i) The *Israel of God* could be the same people as those upon whom the blessing has just been invoked, namely those who live by the principle of the irrelevance of circumcision. It is they who are the true Israel (so for example Betz, p. 322). In Greek there is the word *kai* ('and'/'even'/'also') immediately before *Israel*; on this interpretation it must mean 'even'. Although REB omits the word, its translation of the whole verse seems to imply 'even'. On this reading there is no blessing on historical Israel as such, so that non-Christian Jews are implicitly excluded.

(ii) The *Israel of God* could, by way of complete contrast, be historical Israel, so that Paul is extending the blessing beyond those who accept the irrelevance of circumcision. In this case *kai* must mean 'and also': blessing is invoked both on those *who take this principle for their guide* and also upon *the Israel of God*, i.e. the unbelieving Jews. This interpretation fits well with Paul's refusal to regard historical Israel as irretrievably lost in Rom. 9–11 (see especially 11.26). It also accords with the view of those who think that in the NT 'Israel' never refers to the church, but always to historical Israel.[81] There is a difficulty: it may seem odd that after arguing strenuously throughout the letter against Judaizing, he should at the end bless the Judaizers. This difficulty is not, however, as serious as it initially seems, for what he has been objecting to is not Judaism in itself but only the imposition of Judaism upon Gentile converts (cf. v. 15).

The second of these interpretations seems more in line with Paul's normal usage. We may just note that it has been suggested that we should split the blessing up: peace is invoked on those who accept the unimportance of circumcision, and mercy is invoked on Israel. This has the merit of explaining the very unusual nature of the blessing, unlike any other in Paul's letters but showing similarities to the nineteenth of the Jewish benedictions (of uncertain date: for details see Betz, pp. 321f.).[82] The whole blessing is thus not a straightforward invocation of both peace and mercy to the same group of people. While this explanation cannot be ruled out, it is a far from obvious way of taking the verse.

6.17 *the marks of Jesus branded on my body*: *marks* are *ta stigmata*, which later came to refer to the literal reappearance of the wounds of Jesus in the hands and feet of certain saints. It is most unlikely that the term had such a meaning at this early date. The most immediate explanation of the *marks* is that they are the scars of the beatings and other punishments that he has endured, see II Cor. 11.23–33, and especially vv. 23–25. The main alternative possibility is that he is speaking figuratively of the brand marks of a slave, representing his servanthood to Jesus Christ, cf. II Cor. 4.10, 11. In this case this reference belongs with the passages about dying with, or being crucified with Christ, cf. v. 14.

6.18   *The grace of our Lord Jesus Christ*: a neat reminder of the invocation of grace at the beginning of the letter, 1.3. This ending is virtually identical with that of Philippians (4.23) and that of Philemon (25). See also Rom. 16.20; I Cor. 16.23; II Cor. 13.13; I Thess. 5.28; II Thess. 3.18.

be with you: literally 'be with your spirit', 'spirit' being in the singular. The fact that it is not plural may indicate their oneness in the Spirit of God, who unites them and in whom they live severally and together (cf. I Cor. 12.12–31).

Amen: in Hebrew and Aramaic this is usually the response made by hearers. It may therefore not have been part of the original text, but the pious response of the congregations when the reading of the letter in worship was complete. In view of the harsh tone of some parts of this letter, one can only wonder how heartfelt this *Amen* was on some lips.

ESSAY I

Galatians then and now

Throughout this commentary the aim has been to understand the letter in its contemporary setting, to identify as accurately as possible the problem from which it arose, and to hear what Paul said, as far as we could with the ears of the first hearers. Yet we are men and women of the twentieth century, not the first, and the problems of the churches of Galatia are not exactly our problems. Why then should we continue to read this ancient letter, and if we think that its position in the canon of the New Testament is sufficient answer to that question, *how* should we read it and what may we expect to gain from it?

It would be much easier if we were to continue to hold the view that Galatians is about salvation by the grace of God as opposed to salvation by human merit, by 'good works', for that is something that is always relevant to the human condition. The Reformation knew that. However, in our introductory section we started by rejecting that view of the subject of the letter, and proposed instead that 'What Galatians is about' is fundamentally what is sufficient and necessary to become and remain the people of God: adherence to the Torah and observance of its requirements, or faith in Jesus Christ. As full observance of the Torah is hardly an issue for the vast majority of modern Christians, does this make the letter irrelevant to us in its main thrust, whatever benefit we may gain from it incidentally or in some of its details?[83] Many passages speak today as much as they ever did, e.g. the 'works of the flesh' and the 'fruit of the Spirit' in chapter 5, but do we have to wrench them out of their context in the letter in order to benefit from them?

The crux comes with justification by faith. As usually preached and taught, this is in opposition to justification by works: it is a question of whether we are accepted by God on the grounds of what we do ('works') or on the grounds of faith in Jesus Christ, at its root a simple response, a saying 'yes' to the divine offer of acceptance. This opposition of two ways to God is different from that assumed in this commentary, different not in what Paul is affirming but in what he is denying. No doubt Paul would have been against any idea of justification by human merit, but that was not his target in Galatians (or in Romans). His target was rather the adding of a further requirement to faith in Christ, namely circumcision and what it entails, the observance of the Torah. There is in fact nothing in Galatians to support the fear that doing the law leads to self-righteousness, or 'boasting' before God. There is equally nothing in Galatians to support the view that good works are a problem. They are never attacked in this letter, nor anywhere else in the Pauline letters. His attack on the imposition of the law is not because it might lead to self-righteousness. Rather, its imposition on Gentile Christians is opposed for the following reasons.

(i) Christ and faith in him crucified is all that is needed to enter and remain within the people of God, cf. 1.4; 2.15–21; 4.1–11. That this is so is witnessed to by the Galatians' possession of the Spirit without acceptance of the Torah, 3.1–5. Of course this faith is one that works in life, especially in terms of love, 5.6.

(ii) Where the law separates Jews from Gentiles (2.11ff.), faith unites them, as children of Abraham, 3.6–18, 26–29.

(iii) Although the law did have a subordinate function in the divine economy, that was for an interim period only, a period which is now over, 3.19–29. Similarly the very covenant on Sinai, in comparison with the Abrahamic covenant, is relegated in importance, 4.21–31.

(iv) Where the law leads to curse on those who are not diligent in observing it, the way of faith leads to universal blessing, 3.10–14.

(v) Perhaps we could add the insuperable difficulty of observing the law fully (3.11), but we have argued that this is probably an aspect of (ii) and refers not to the difficulty Jews find, but to the problems Gentiles would have in keeping it.

Now all this is anchored very firmly in the time when the church was working out its own identity in relation to Judaism: was it a continuation of Judaism, a sect within it, a totally new religion, or what? Although there is not much sign in Galatians that this was a concrete social problem, apart from chapter 2 and the Antioch incident, common sense tells us that it was not merely theoretical. There must at least in some parts of Galatia have been a synagogue nearby: did some Christians belong to that as well as to the Christian community, or did they not? It they did, they would need to remain in good standing with it, and the narration of the affair at Antioch would surely have been given by Paul as a parallel case and an object lesson. His answer to the issues raised by such a situation constitutes the Epistle to the Galatians, and there is little doubt that the nub of his position consists in (i) and (ii) above.[84] First, nothing must compete with Christ as the necessary *and sufficient* ground of salvation; faith in him is all that is needed on the human side. Secondly, circumcision and the consequent obligation to observe the law are specifically Jewish, and to require these of Gentile converts is to say that only Jews, or those who are willing to become Jews, can be within God's people. Faith, on the other hand, is potentially universal: all those who have faith like that of Abraham are his true children, whether they be Jews or Gentiles.

We thus see that Paul was aiming at a target substantially different from that of someone like Luther. Paul was not fighting against a merit-centred religion or against self-righteousness, though had they been problems to him he would doubtless have opposed both. He was against not 'good works' but specifically 'works of the law', above all for the two reasons just given. So, to repeat the question, what happens to justification by faith if we conclude that what Paul was attacking was substantially different from what was attacked by classic Protestantism, even if what he affirmed was the same?

We could argue that nothing much need change. The basic idea of justification by faith does not depend on Paul alone, let alone solely on the letter to the Galatians. It is implicit in the gospels' portrayal of Jesus as consorting and eating with sinners, without first demanding that they repent. It is explicit in the parable of the Pharisee and the Publican (Luke 18.9–14), which is indeed aimed at self-righteousness. Even in Paul's writings, the same fundamental teaching could be derived not through his justification language but from passages about redemption or reconciliation, see for instance Rom. 5.10; Gal. 1.3–4; 4.5, 8–9. In any case, we could argue that centuries of Christian history have done quite enough to establish the doctrine, and we need not be too worried if Paul's letters in general and Galatians in particular turn out to be aimed at something other than justification by good works. Justification by faith is after all congruent with the nature of God and his dealings with humanity as set out in the Bible as a whole.

There is something in all this. The trouble is that we *do have* the Epistle to the Galatians, and it does have a long history of contributing to the doctrine of justification as a central tenet of Christianity. We cannot easily ignore it therefore, and in any case the modern reader needs to have some notion of what to do with it. Moreover it would now be very difficult to continue discussing justification while ignoring Paul and the Pauline passages that concern it. The terminology is so much his terminology and the history of the question is so much the history of the interpretation of the Pauline material. Further, it is not as if Paul in the interpretation we have adopted, and Paul in the traditional interpretation, were diametrically opposed. To repeat, the difficulty is not in what he is affirming about justification by faith but in what he is affirming it against. Not only, therefore, would it be difficult to remove Paul from the discussion of the subject, it would be unnecessary and even a little eccentric.

This commentary is written by one who happens to think that a Christianity without justification by faith would be well-nigh intolerable. That is to say that we need (at its simplest) a doctrine which, at the end of the day, literally at the Last Day, tells us that our acceptance with God does not depend upon our deserving it. Otherwise we must all fear that we are irretrievably lost. If we are now told that in its earliest explicit form this doctrine does not say quite what we thought, where are we?

Two solutions may be suggested, the first of which will be passed over very rapidly because it has much more relevance to Romans than to Galatians. Stephen Westerholm[85] has argued that Paul's rejection of works of the law for salvation is the particular instance, in his time and culture, of the rejection of any kind of works for salvation. Paul sets doing and believing in polar opposition. There is a little to justify this suggestion in Romans (see 4.2), but it does not seem to accord well with the main thrust of the argument even there. So far as one can see, there is nothing at all to support it in Galatians, and we shall therefore say no more about it.[86]

The other solution to the dilemma is to use the way of analogy: this may be an inexact use of the word, but it is hard to think of a more appropriate alternative. The suggestion is this: the role played by 'good works' in the traditional Lutheran and Protestant exegesis of Paul is analogous to the role played by 'works of the law' in Paul's own day. There is nothing wrong or even unusual in making something in the interpreter's situation analogous to something in a writer's text. Those who use ancient texts to speak to their own time regularly and almost inevitably work to a degree by analogy. The attack of Jesus or Paul or Amos or Isaiah on something in his own day and his own society is kept pretty much unchanged, but switched from its ancient target to a modern one, but one which has enough in common with the ancient target to make the switch plausible.

Obviously the results can be grotesque or trivial, but they can also be of great moment. The point is not only that this switch can happen, but also that it has to happen unless we are to transport ourselves back into the world of the ancient text not as visitors but as residents. Therefore whenever we interpret the Bible in other than a strictly antiquarian way we are working to some extent by analogy.

In our present case it is not difficult to see why the analogy should work. We have noted that Paul rejects the imposition of the law as a régime on his Gentile converts for two chief reasons: (i) Christianity must be universal, and not just for Jews or Jewish converts; and (ii) if justification is by faith in Christ, then nothing further must be demanded, no supplement and certainly no alternative. It is especially this second reason that is prominent in Galatians: there can be no competitor nor supplement to faith in Christ, e.g. 1.7; 2.21; 3.3, 6–18, 23–29; even the Sarah-Hagar piece, 4.21–31, underlines the alternative nature of Christ and the law. It is, however, particularly in 5.1–6 that Christ and faith on the one hand, and circumcision and law on the other hand, are set out as alternatives. Of course Paul considers the second alternative to be no real option at all. The core of the matter is in 5.4:

> When you seek to be justified by way of law, you are cut off from Christ: you have put yourselves outside God's grace.

In Paul's eyes the only necessary and sufficient condition for salvation is faith in Jesus Christ, through whom God's grace has been definitively expressed. All other things may or may not be useful or valuable but they are neither central nor essential (cf. 6.15 on circumcision). Justification cannot be by faith *and* something else, otherwise Christ is removed from the centre, and otherwise the extra requirement would discriminate in favour of some and against others. Adding circumcision discriminates in favour of Jews and against Gentiles: this was the issue in Paul's day.

We may say again that the extra requirement of circumcision and the consequent obligation to live by the Torah have not been live issues for most Christians for many centuries. There may, however, be other 'extra requirements', and for Luther and the Protestant tradition in particular the demand for good works fell into this category. To require good works, which would overlap with works of the law but would be by no means identical with them, was to impugn the sufficiency and centrality of Jesus Christ and of faith in him. We are talking, of course, about good works as a condition of acceptance, not as its consequence. The 'Lutheran' exegesis of Paul thus worked analogically to the rejection of works of the law in favour of faith: for such exegetes it was rejection of good works. It was working on a parallel case, one relevant to their own time as rejecting works of the law was not. There is nothing wrong in this: if one, then not the other, but not *any other at all*, not works of the law, but not good works either. The only mistake would be to fail to recognize that analogy was in operation, and to believe that Paul's target in the first century was identical with the target of the sixteenth and later centuries. Many now believe that this mistake was made, leading both to mistaken exegesis of Paul and to erroneous historical judgments about the Judaism of Paul's time.

Yet this switching of targets would have been entirely legitimate if it had stayed within its proper bounds, as exposition rather than exegesis, i.e. recognizing that a somewhat different target was replacing the original one, in the interests of letting the ancient text speak to a different day and a different situation. Paul was not talking about good works as an alternative to faith in Christ, but as he clearly believed that there was *no* alternative to that faith, Luther and his followers were entitled to propose good works as another such non-alternative.

Perhaps it all boils down to this: in using Paul and in particular his Letter to the Galatians when we talk about justification by faith, we ought not to forget the difference between Paul's target and the one traditional in Western Christendom. We are entitled to let the letter speak to our time, our needs and our society if it will, and we need make no apology for that. What we are not entitled to do is make Paul say what he does not say, and above all to make historical judgments about the Jews for which we have no historical evidence. Galatians is not about Christian faith as the answer to a self-righteous, merit-centred, Jewish religion: so far as we know, those are not things of which the Judaism of the time could be accused. Nevertheless if we in our society have any tendency to be self-righteous, or merit-centred, or overly influenced by a secular environment heavily oriented towards achievement, then Paul's arguments to the Galatian churches may speak to our condition as much as they ever did to men and women in the first or the sixteenth century.

ESSAY II

Galatians: historical questions

We have said that the aim of the commentary has been to help the modern reader to hear what Paul was saying with the ear of a first-century hearer. Because the twentieth century is our time, such a reader also has an ear of his or her own, and the commentator hopes that here and there and particularly in Essay I, he has done a little to encourage the use of that ear.

By design, matters that are of mainly historical interest have been treated only lightly. Yet although the issues covered in this present essay on the whole affect only slightly the reading and understanding of the letter, there is something to be said for having a grasp of what they are. In most cases the solutions to the problems are far from agreed.

1. Who were the Galatians?

At the time of Paul, the term 'Galatia' could be used for two overlapping geographical and political entities.

(i) There was the old kingdom of Galatia, ruled by Celts who had settled there about three centuries before Paul's time. This was an area on the central Anatolian plain, around Ancyra (modern Ankara).

(ii) There was the Roman province of Galatia which included the old Celtic kingdom, and whose precise boundaries varied from time to time, but which in Paul's day included Phrygian and Lycaonian areas in the south of Asia Minor.

The discussion on this issue is endless. In favour of the Roman province (sometimes called the South Galatian theory) is that Acts tells us that Paul did visit cities there, including Derbe and Lystra (see Acts 13–14). 'South Galatia' is strictly speaking a misnomer, since it covered an area from the Black Sea to the southern coast of modern Turkey, but the appellation is used because it is the southern part of it that we know Paul to have visited, at least according to Acts.

111

We do not know when he visited the churches of the central plain ('North Galatia) if indeed he ever did (though see Acts 16.6; 18.23).

Against 'South Galatia' is that the Phrygians and Lycaonians were not normally (some would say not ever) referred to as 'Galatians': Grayston (p. 13) points out that for Paul to call them Galatians would have been as tactless as for the Secretary of the World Council of churches in the mid-twentieth century to address the Christians of Latvia, Estonia and Lithuania as 'you foolish Russians'.

One complication about identifying the destination of the letter is that matters of dating, and therefore of relationships with Acts and with the other letters, are tied up with it. If 'Galatia' is primarily the southern area, Derbe, Lystra and so on, then Galatians could have been written soon after his visit there and before the so-called Apostolic Council of Acts 15. This would solve, or partly solve, the problem of the relation between Acts 15 and Gal. 2 (see 4. below). If Galatia is the old Celtic kingdom, then presumably Paul visited it after the Council (Acts 16.6) and then again later (Acts 18.23). This leaves us with the problem why Paul does not mention the Council's decree, with its waiving of the requirement of circumcision for Gentile converts. On the other hand it puts the date of Galatians nearer that of Romans, the letter with which it has most in common in subject matter and treatment. Most readers may feel that they can live without having this whole issue resolved, but they ought to be aware the issue exists, and indeed has a bearing on the next topic.

2. *The social setting of the Galatian churches*

It is obvious that to treat Paul's letters as disembodied theological treatises, unrelated to the social composition of the society and the church to which they were addressed, is to distort them. Much fruitful work is now being done to put the Pauline writings in their sociological contexts. Sometimes this is easier (as in the case of the Corinthian correspondence, and even in the case of Romans) than it is here. Our inability to be sure where Galatia was carries with it the inability to know whether they were Celts, once but no longer the political masters, or Celts assimilated to an older culture, or indigenous but Hellenized peoples of other sorts. Betz (pp. 2–3) has an hypothesis that they were the Hellenized townspeople of the old Galatian kingdom: he is sure that the 'North Galatian' theory is correct, and then argues from the intricate rhetorical nature of the letter that Paul was writing to highly educated people. Yet this assumes that what Paul wrote was adapted to his readership/ audience, an assumption that is hard to sustain with confidence; who has not listened to a sermon in which a preacher tacitly but quite wrongly imputes to a congregation a level of learning that they simply do not have? In other words Paul may have written over the heads of his readers (see II Peter 3.16) theologically, and have treated them as enjoying a level of culture that was in fact beyond them. We simply do not know whether they were highly educated, relatively privileged people, or not. We do not know whether there were many slaves, or slave-owners, among them or not. We do not know for sure whether the issue over the law was a social one, involving relations with putative local synagogues, or was purely a matter of how the Christian communities themselves ordered their own existence. If Galatia included Derbe and Lystra, then Acts 14 tells us that there were Jews about, but if the churches were in the central Anatolian plain, we do not know how commonly synagogues were to be found. On the whole it seems likely that the point of Paul's narration of the Antioch incident in Gal. 2 is that there were similar pressures from those who wanted to maintain fellowship with the Jewish community in Antioch and Galatia, and that we may infer local synagogues, but we cannot be sure.

Francis Watson[87] however is nearer the mark when he identifies the issue in Galatia as whether the Christian church was to be a 'reform-movement within the Jewish community' or a body (Watson uses the word 'sect') that did not follow the distinctive patterns of conduct of Judaism and that had a predominantly Gentile membership. Whether or not we think that sect-terminology is appropriate, Watson's analysis of the situation seems to fit the letter Paul wrote. Are Christians Jews of a sort, or are they some new species? Gal. 6.15 answers this question: they are a new creation. This stands whether or not there were synagogues round the corner from where the Christians met.

3. Paul's opponents in Galatia

By now it must be clear that those whose views Paul aims to rebut were Judaizers of some sort. That they were basically Gnostics, who merely wanted to impose circumcision as a mystic ritual, without also requiring the observance of the Torah as a whole, is a view that may derive some support from 5.3 (the Galatians needed to be told that circumcision entails full Torah-observance)[88], but it founders on the fact that Paul's rebuttal is aimed not against just one or two items of the law, but against the law as a whole, e.g. 4.21. It is conceivable that the opponents were neither Jews nor Jewish Christians but Gentile Christians who, perhaps, had heard or read parts of the Septuagint and had concluded that circumcision was necessary for full membership of the people of God, or had made contact with the local synagogue and had been told the same by practising Jews.[89] The difficulty with this suggestion is that the first two chapters of Galatians are devoted to clarifying Paul's relation to the Jerusalem church, which seems to indicate that somewhere in that direction was where the trouble lay. Moreover, the Antioch incident also indicates that the issue was in general the relation between the church and Judaism, and once again Jerusalem comes into the picture.

If it is most likely, therefore, that the troublemakers were some Jewish Christians, it is none the less striking that Paul never says that they were emissaries of, or came with the authority of, James and the church of Jerusalem. In the light of his reported rebuke to Peter (2.11–14) he would surely not have hesitated to attack James if he thought that the Jerusalem church was the source of his difficulties with Galatia. Further, we should have expected much less politeness about Jerusalem in 2.1–10 than in fact we find. It seems most probable that Paul's opponents, though no doubt believing that they were in line with the mother church of Jerusalem, did not have that church's authorization.

4. *The so-called Council of Jerusalem: Galatians 2 and Acts 15*

A casual reader of these two chapters might very well conclude that, although there were differences between them, they referred to the same occasion. Both concern the necessity or otherwise of circumcision for Gentile converts. Both take place in Jerusalem. Both involve Paul and Barnabas on the one side, and the Jerusalem apostles and leaders, including James, on the other. Both conclude that circumcision is not to be required.

Among other differences, such as the presence of Titus in Gal. 2 but not in Acts 15, there are two crucial ones. First, in Acts this is Paul's third visit to Jerusalem after becoming a Christian (the second is in 11.29f.), while in Galatians Paul gives considerable emphasis to the fact that it is only his second. Secondly, in Galatians the only condition laid upon the Gentile churches is that they 'remember the poor', which presumably means that they promise to support the Jerusalem Christians financially. In Acts 15.20, 29 however there is an 'Apostolic Decree' which lays down what look like dietary restrictions to be observed by Gentile converts. There is a textual variant which makes the list of requirements look more like fundamentally moral demands; even if the list is dietary, it can be held that it is aimed more at avoiding contamination with idolatry than at keeping specifically Jewish rules[90], but the usual interpretation is that the decree was intended to enable Jewish Christians to eat with Gentile Christians without religious scruples. Now there is no mention of this decree by Paul, in Galatians or anywhere else. Are these two accounts, therefore, different and perhaps equally tendentious reports of the same event, or do they describe different occasions?

Major books of New Testament Introduction and full-scale commentaries on both Acts and Galatians explore this issue at length. Here we can make only a few comments.

(i) We can solve the problem of the number of visits by supposing that Galatians is written very early, between the visits of Acts 11 and Acts 15. This explains why Paul does not talk about a full-scale Council: it has not yet happened. It requires us to suppose that the 'famine visit' of Acts 11.29f. was much more than that: it did not involve a full Council like that of Acts 15, but there was a more private meeting, consistent with the story in Gal. 2, at which the issue of circumcision was discussed. Acts has simply omitted any mention of this meeting; this is not a problem, as the author paints with a wide brush and leaves many gaps in his story of the early church.[91]

There are two serious difficulties with this view and one slight drawback. The first difficulty is it supposes two quite similar meetings, so similar that our casual reader thinks they are identical. The second difficulty is that many scholars find it hard to believe that Paul would ever have agreed to the list of dietary restrictions, if that is what they are, laid out in Acts 15.20, 29. He would probably, for instance, have had to retract his rebuke to Peter (Gal. 2.11, 14) who was surely only doing what the decree said he ought to do, at least by implication. It is also strange that in I Cor. 8, 10 and Rom. 14 he discusses different habits of diet, including the eating of food offered to idols, specifically banned by the decree, without showing any awareness of the decision supposedly agreed at Jerusalem after the writing of Galatians but before the writing of I Corinthians and Romans. Indeed what he says in those letters is hardly consistent with that decision. Either, then, he later regretted his assent to the Jerusalem decree or he was never a party to it. The latter seems more likely. This problem is not solved by making the Acts 15 meeting subsequent to that of Gal. 2.

The slight drawback is that if Galatians was written before the Council of Acts 15, then it is a very early letter, and well removed in time from the strikingly similar Romans. It also must then surely have been written to 'south Galatia', to people in Derbe, Lystra and so on. If we accept the order of events in Acts as being broadly correct, Paul did not go near the old kingdom of Galatia until after the Council, 16.6; 18.23. If on other grounds we think he wrote to the old Celtic kingdom, a date before the Council for the writing of Galatians becomes less likely.

(ii) Much of what has been said under (i) assumes the basic historical reliability of Acts. If we begin to doubt that, then recon-struction of what happened becomes more difficult. Yet recon-struction will become easier if we opt for a different sort of solution, namely that Paul is right in his account, and that Gal. 2 and Acts 15 do describe the same event, but that there was no decree, that it was Paul's second and not his third visit to Jerusalem after his conver-sion, so that even if Acts is correct in broad outline it is in detail mistaken. In particular, the Acts 11.29 visit could be identical with that of Acts 15, wrongly separated by 'Luke'; more importantly, though there may well have been a decree like that found in Acts 15.20, it came from a later time and Paul had no part in its formula-tion or dissemination.

(iii) There are many varieties of these two solutions, and further proposals as well, but what we have said will give some idea of the issues at stake. It must be confessed that the interpretation of Gal. 2 is not in itself much affected by this whole problem. It matters much more for students of Acts, and for the reconstruction of the history of the earliest church.

5. *Authorship*

With so many things uncertain (date, destination, and the identity of the opponents) it may be a relief to know that there is virtually no dispute about authorship. It is true that it has been argued that Galatians as we have it is not the Galatians Paul wrote: in 1972 J. C. O'Neill attempted to show that many of the difficulties in the letter are to be explained by postulating that it has been glossed and interpolated by later hands.[92] Even he, however, thinks that the bulk of the letter is authentically Pauline. He has an acute eye for difficulties in sense and logic, but most commentaries (including this one) assume that it is more likely that Paul sometimes wrote with less than perfect clarity – or even consistency – than that O'Neill's theory of glosses and interpolations is correct.

NOTES

1. K. Stendahl, *Paul Among Jews and Gentiles*, SCM Press 1977.
2. E. P. Sanders, *Paul and Palestinian Judaism*, SCM Press 1977; *Paul, the Law, and the Jewish People*, Fortress 1983, SCM Press 1985.
3. See for example J. Smit, 'The Letter of Paul to the Galatians: a Deliberative Speech', *NTS* 35, 1989, 1–26, and the critical survey in G. W. Hansen, *Abraham in Galatians*, Sheffield Academic Press 1989, Part I; also Fung, pp. 28–32.
4. For recent discussion of this see K. Grayston, *Dying, We Live*, Darton, Longman and Todd 1990, pp. 69, 80, 306.
5. The Greek translation of the Old Testament and Apocrypha, usually cited as LXX.
6. There could be occasional exceptions if the reason was good. See the case of King Izates of Adiabene (Josephus, *Ant.* 20.38ff.) and discussion in Alan F. Segal, *Paul the Convert*, Yale University Press 1990, pp. 99–101.
7. See J. Munck, *Paul and the Salvation of Mankind*, SCM Press 1959, pp. 87ff., 131f.
8. See W. Schmithals, *Paul and the Gnostics*, Abingdon 1972, pp. 13–64.
9. For the first, see H. Räisänen, *The Torah and Christ*, Finnish Exegetical Society 1986, ch. III; for the second, S. Kim, *The Origin of Paul's Gospel*, J. C. B. Mohr (Paul Siebeck), ²1984.
10. See Stendahl, *Paul Among Jews and Gentiles*, pp. 7–22: 'Call rather than Conversion'. Contrast Segal, *Paul the Convert*, pp. 5–8 and often.
11. For further discussion see J. A. Ziesler, *Pauline Christianity*, OUP ²1990, pp. 49–65.
12. So Segal, *Paul the Convert*, pp. 129, 194–210, and *passim*. It is noteworthy that although some discussions of the Noachic laws are later, that in *Jubilees* is pre-Christian.
13. So J. Paul Sampley, *Pauline Partnership in Christ*, Fortress 1980, ch. III.

14. See B. Byrne, '*Sons of God*' – '*Seed of Abraham*', Biblical Institute Press, Rome 1979, p. 143.
15. For an account of the possibilities see J. D. G. Dunn, *Jesus, Paul and the Law*, SPCK 1990, ch. VI.
16. See E. P. Sanders, *Jewish Law from Jesus to the Mishnah*, SCM Press/Trinity Press International 1990, ch. IV; idem., *Jesus and Judaism*, SCM Press 1985, ch. VI and especially pp. 180–211, about Jesus but with implications for our passage. There seem to have been two views on this question: see *Jub.* 22.16 and P. J. Tomson, *Paul and the Jewish Law*, Van Gorcum/Fortress 1990, pp. 230–236.
17. See for example J. Daniélou, *The Theology of Jewish Christianity*, Darton, Longman and Todd 1964, pp. 55–64.
18. See N. Turner, *Christian Words*, T. & T. Clark 1980, p. 219.
19. So Dunn, *Jesus, Paul and the Law*, pp. 191–4.
20. With Sanders, *Paul and the Palestinian Judaism*, p. 501, contrast Dunn, *Jesus, Paul and the Law*, p. 190.
21. See Grayston, *Dying, We Live*, pp. 73, 86.
22. As by Dunn, *Jesus, Paul and the Law*, pp. 195–8.
23. For a recent and spirited defence of this view see M. D. Hooker, *From Adam to Christ*, CUP 1990, ch. 14.
24. See J. A. Ziesler, *The Meaning of Righteousness in Paul*, CUP 1972, chs. X and XI, and for this specific point, pp. 180, 208f.
25. So Dunn, *Jesus, Paul and the Law*, pp. 191–5. For counter-argument see Räisänen, *Torah and Christ*, ch. VII.
26. See Grayston, *Dying, We Live*, p. 72.
27. So C. F. D. Moule, *The Phenomenon of the New Testament*, SCM Press 1967, pp. 22–26.
28. For example, M. Hengel, *The Son of God*, SCM Press 1976; J. D. G. Dunn, *Christology in the Making*, SCM Press 1980, pp. 12–64; *TDNT*, pp. 1206–15.
29. Cf. Ziesler, *Meaning of Righteousness*, p. 174.
30. See M. E. Isaacs, *The Concept of Spirit*, Heythrop 1976, pp. 82–96.
31. The meaning of *sarx* has a rich literature. For an excellent analysis see J. M. G. Barclay, *Obeying the Truth*, T. & T. Clark 1988, ch. VI.
32. There is a long and useful discussion in Fung, pp. 130–33.
33. So C. K. Barrett, *Essays on Paul*, SPCK 1982, pp. 158f.
34. For example Ecclus. 44.19–21; *Jub.* 23.10; 24.11; *II Apoc. Bar.* 57.2.
35. See N. A. Dahl, 'The Atonement – Adequate Reward for Akedah?' in *Neotestamentica et Semitica*, ed. E. E. Ellis and M. Wilcox, T. & T. Clark 1969, pp. 15–29.

36. For possible links with Hellenistic Jewish use of Abraham see Betz, p. 139.

37. Contrast Sanders, *Paul, the Law, and the Jewish People*, pp. 20–24, with H. Räisänen, *Paul and the Law*, J. C. B. Mohr (Paul Siebeck) 1983, pp. 94–6.

38. See Hooker, *From Adam to Christ*, pp. 14–16, 33, 170–72 (and also Bruce, ad loc). This is one of Hooker's notable examples of 'interchange in Christ'.

39. So Grayston, *Dying, We Live*, p. 79.

40. See Ziesler, *Meaning of Righteousness*, pp. 180–85; also Bruce, p. 153.

41. So S. Westerholm, *Israel's Law and the Church's Faith*, Eerdmans 1988, pp. 111–13.

42. See *TDNT*, pp. 157–61. Note that Philo uses *synthēkē* for 'treaty' and reserves *diathēkē* for the divine 'disposing' (p. 160). For fuller discussion of the difficulties of Paul's illustration see Betz, pp. 154–6.

43. Cf. Byrne, *'Sons of God'*, pp. 156f., 160f.

44. It is also doubtful if this is what the Romans passages are saying; see J. A. Ziesler, 'The Role of the Tenth Commandment in Romans 7', *JSNT* 33, 1988, 41–56.

45. See Grayston, *Dying, We Live*, pp. 78f.: the Torah works like a safety fence.

46. See N. H. Young, *'Paidagogos*: the Social Setting of a Pauline Metaphor', *NT* xxix, 1987, 150–76.

47. Cf. Rom. 13.14; Col. 310; Eph. 4.24. For the rich contemporary background to the language of 'putting off' and 'putting on' see Betz, pp. 188f.; Bonnard pp. 78, 153.

48. On the whole complex of ideas see Byrne, *'Sons of God'*, especially ch. III.

49. See Dunn, *Christology in the Making*, pp. 38–44 for discussion and further references.

50. Cf. Hooker's treatment of 'interchange in Christ', *From Adam to Christ*, chs. I–IV; also Byrne, op. cit., pp. 178–86.

51. See G. Vermes, *Jesus the Jew*, Fortress/SCM Press 1983, pp. 210–13, who moderates the somewhat exaggerated treatment by J. Jeremias, *New Testament Theology* I, SCM Press 1971, pp. 36f., 61–68.

52. Though see Schmithals, *Paul and the Gnostics*, pp. 13–64.

53. See W. M. Ramsay, *St Paul the Traveller and Roman Citizen*,

Hodder & Stoughton 11th edition, 1912, p. 192 (the year 54–55), altered on p. xxxi of the 14th edition, 1920, to 47–48.

54. C. K. Barrett seems to consider the possibility a real one, 'Pauline Controversies in the Post-Pauline Period', *NTS* 20, 1974, 229–245, at 230f.

55. See J. A. Ziesler, *Paul's Letter to the Romans*, SCM Press/Trinity Press International 1989, pp. 118–20.

56. For some details see Bruce, pp. 223f. In Josephus, *Ant.* 1.215 we find fears that Ishmael would harm Isaac.

57. So Barrett, *Essays on Paul*, p. 165.

58. Cf. Barclay, *Truth*, p. 64: the Galatians may have been simply naive. Similarly Bruce, pp. 229–31.

59. See Sanders, *Paul, the Law, and the Jewish People*, pp. 27–9.

60. See Turner, *Christian Words*, pp. 213–15; *TDNT*, pp. 229–32.

61. Cf. Ziesler, *Meaning of Righteousness*, pp. 179f., 209.

62. So G.Howard, *Paul: Crisis in Galatia*, CUP 1979, pp. 10, 39, 44.

63. So F. Watson, *Paul, Judaism and the Gentiles*, CUP 1986, pp. 28–31.

64. For this view see most famously J. H. Ropes, *The Singular Problem of the Epistle to the Galatians*, Harvard Theological Studies 1929.

65. See Barclay, *Truth*, pp. 68–72, 106–45 and passim (summary on p. 218).

66. Gal. 1.4; 2.4; 3.13, 22–25; 4.1–10, 21–31; 5.1. For a stimulating study of Galatians from this angle see C. K. Barrett, *Freedom and Obligation*, SPCK 1985.

67. See also Barclay, *Truth*, pp. 153–5.

68. So Barclay, *Truth*, pp. 124f.

69. Following Barclay, *Truth*, pp. 138–141.

70. See Barclay, *Truth*, pp. 112–16, who also gives a useful survey of the possibilities.

71. See further Turner, *Christian Words*, pp. 261–6; *TDNT*, pp. 5–10.

72. See further *TDNT*, pp. 1299–1301.

73. Turner, *Christian Words*, pp. 320f.; *TDNT*, pp. 207–11.

74. Barclay, *Truth*, pp. 124–5.

75. See especially Betz, pp. 291–311, but also the critical comments of Barclay, *Truth*, pp. 170–77.

76. Quoted from Barclay, *Truth*, p. 134.

77. Strictly speaking the two verbs are not the same: we have *anaplēroō* here but *plēroō* in 5.14. Nevertheless it would almost certainly be a mistake to try to detect some subtle difference between them.

78. For a good and succint discussion of the issue see Howard, *Paul: Crisis in Galatia*, pp. 17–19.
79. See Schmithals, *Paul and the Gnostics*, pp. 13–64.
80. On the Romans passage see Ziesler, *Romans*, pp. 218–21.
81. See especially P. Richardson, *Israel in the Apostolic Church*, CUP 1969.
82. For this suggestion see Richardson, op. cit., pp. 81–4.
83. I have explored this issues at greater length in 'Justification by Faith in the Light of the "New Perspectives on Paul"', *Theology* May 1991. I am grateful to the editors for permission to use substantial parts of the article in the present essay.
84. See Sanders, *Paul, the Law, and the Jewish People*, ch. II.
85. S. Westerholm, *Israel's Law and the Church's Faith*, pp. 111–30.
86. I have discussed it a little more fully in the article cited in n.83.
87. F. Watson, *Paul, Judaism and the Gentiles*, pp. 49–72.
88. See Schmithals, *Paul and the Gnostics*, pp. 13–64.
89. See Munck, *Paul and the Salvation of Mankind*, pp. 87ff., 131f.
90. See S. G. Wilson, *Luke and the Law*, CUP 1983, pp. 73–102.
91. For this theory see further Fung, pp. 9–28.
92. J. C. O'Neill, *The Recovery of Paul's Letter to the Galatians*, SPCK.